Regis!

Regis!

The Unauthorized Biography

KATHLEEN TRACY

The publication of *Regis! The Unauthorized Biography* has been generously
supported by the Government of Canada through
the Book Publishing Industry Development Program.

© ECW PRESS, 2000.

CANADIAN CATALOGUING IN PUBLICATION DATA

Tracy, Kathleen
Regis!: the unauthorized biography

Includes bibliographical references.
ISBN 1-55022-439-5

1. Philbin, Regis. 2. Television personalities –
United States – Biography. I. Title.
PN1992.4.P45T72 2001 791.45'028'092 C00-932378-3

Front cover photo by Josef Astor / Outline.
Copyedited by Dallas Harrison.
Cover and interior design by Guylaine Régimbald – SOLO DESIGN.
Typesetting by Yolande Martel.
This book is set in Minion and Nueva.

Printed by Transcontinental.

Distributed in Canada by General Distribution Services,
325 Humber College Boulevard, Etobicoke, Ontario M9W 7C3.

Distributed in the United States by LPC Group,
1436 West Randolph Street, Chicago, IL 60607, U.S.A.

Distributed in Europe by Turnaround Publisher Services, Unit 3,
Olympia Trading Estate, Coburg Road, Wood Green, London, N2Z 6T2.

Distributed in Australia and New Zealand by Wakefield Press,
17 Rundle Street (Box 2266), Kent Town, South Australia 5071.

Published by ECW PRESS
Suite 200
2120 Queen Street East
Toronto, Ontario M4E 1E2.
ecwpress.com

PRINTED AND BOUND IN CANADA

Contents

Introduction

Sometimes it's all a matter of chemistry – that ultimately indefinable but instantly recognizable magic that happens between two people whose auras align just so. Chemistry is particularly enigmatic because it can happen between two people who don't like each other – some of the most electric on-screen romances in movie history happened between costars whose off-camera animosity crackled.

In the case of Regis Philbin and Kathie Lee Gifford, their on-air chemistry catapulted two journeymen television personalities into the stratosphere of daytime megastars. Prior to their pairing, they'd made names for themselves, but neither had shown any promise of rising above the broadcast multitudes. But together they exuded an edgy energy, and watching them perform their unique early morning verbal dance became an addictive, guilty pleasure for many.

Kathie Lee, after years of threatening to quit *Live! With Regis & Kathie Lee*, finally decided to leave the show – perhaps not so coincidentally – just as Regis became the most watched man on television thanks to the phenomenal success of *Who Wants to Be a Millionaire?* He has decided to continue the morning show for at least another year, while Kathie Lee hopes to conquer prime time with a sitcom of her own.

But whatever paths their careers take from this point on, one thing is indisputable: the unique chemistry between Regis and Kathie Lee was lightning in a bottle, once-in-a-career magic that neither will find again with anyone else.

1

Young "King" Philbin

If Kermit the Frog thinks it isn't easy being green, he should try growing up with a name such as Regis Philbin. "Johnny Carson has made great gags over the years about my name," Regis told Larry Eisenberg in a 1992 *Good Housekeeping* interview. "He said Regis was an English cigarette or a hotel." The only child of Frank and Florence Philbin, Regis was named after the high school Frank had attended, Regis High School, a Jesuit boys' school on the Upper East Side of Manhattan – from which Frank had allegedly been kicked out at one point for fighting. The incident had been only a minor setback, and Frank eventually earned a master's degree at New York University in labor relations. After that, the family moved to Brooklyn for a couple of years before finally settling in the Bronx. And, through it all, Regis – which means "king" – learned to deal with the quizzical looks his name inspired among his peers. "People still ask me, is that your real name?" he admitted to Eisenberg, then deadpanned: "Why would anybody *adopt* a name like Regis Philbin?"

Thanks to Frank's Irish heritage and Florence's Italian heritage, Regis grew up in a strict Catholic household that gave him both discipline and warmth. His mom was "a lot of fun," recalled childhood friend Ed Trerotola to AMI Specials for the magazine

Regis Uncensored. "His lightness came from her. The determination clearly came from his father because his father always impressed me as a tough guy; in the good sense of the word tough guy."

Born on August 25, 1933, on Manhattan's west side at Childs Hospital, Regis was baptized at St. Paul's Cathedral, and in the Bronx he attended Our Lady of Solace Grammar School and later Cardinal Hayes High School. Although the Philbins lived in a modest house with some of his mother's relatives, Regis has only fond memories of his childhood and youth, though he was embarrassed as a boy when his mother encouraged him to slip under subway turnstiles. Among his fondest memories are the times he spent hanging out on local street corners with his buddies. On his own, Regis was often shy and willing to hang in the background, but when he had an audience his showman side came out. Standing on the street corner razzing his friends or joking with passersby, Regis became the life of the party, and his teen years in the Bronx were filled with laughs and good times.

For his parents, the ultimate college education for their son could only be had at Notre Dame. Even though it meant saving nearly every penny he made as a personnel director, Frank Philbin was determined to put his son through the most famous Catholic college in the world – even though Regis would be far from home. Located in South Bend, Indiana, a couple of hours east of Chicago, Notre Dame symbolizes both tough-nosed college football and academic expectations of the highest order. Although fully aware that he was being given a significant opportunity for higher education, Regis felt lonely and like an outsider at the college, where he majored in sociology.

"My college experience is really what changed my life," Regis would comment years later to *People*'s Sue Carswell. "Everything I did at Notre Dame, including the books I read, provided a life-changing experience for me." That said, he is the first to admit he was just an average student, though he scored high marks as a practical joker. "I was always carrying on in the hallways. I used to twist this one kid's feet when he was asleep. I thought it was such a scream."

In an effort to make friends and participate in extracurricular activities, the slender-framed Regis took up intramural boxing while at Notre Dame. Although he had the courage to face an opponent in the ring, he couldn't muster up the fortitude to confront his real desire: television. Throughout his childhood and at college, Regis harbored a secret fascination for the entertainment business. One day, while wandering the campus, he found himself at the college television station. "I just wanted to go inside and see what was going on," he recalled to *Good Housekeeping's* Eisenberg. "I walked over but I could not bring myself to knock on the door so I never went in."

Although Philbin left Notre Dame with unfulfilled dreams, the school remains his "favorite place in the world." In retrospect, he told Carswell, Notre Dame represents "everything that is good and fair and just. I think the world would be a much better place if people adhered to the golden rules of Notre Dame."

After graduating from the university, Regis enlisted in the navy, eventually working his way up to the rank of lieutenant. At the end of his tour, he was based in Coronado, California, just down the coast from Los Angeles, where he thought his dreams of a television career could come true. He finally admitted his seemingly out-of-reach goal to a couple of service buddies prior to his release. Just saying it out loud gave Regis extra confidence that he *could* have a career in television.

So, on the day he was discharged from the navy, Regis drove directly to Los Angeles intent on finally knocking on that door he'd walked away from in college. Even though he had no experience and a résumé that simply listed his sociology degree and his stint in the navy, Regis was undeterred. His plan was to finagle a meeting with ex-marine Al Flanagan, the program director of a local LA television station, KCOP, in the hope of getting hired to do *anything*. He'd gotten Flanagan's name from a movie critic at the *San Diego Union* after simply walking into the newsroom and asking for help getting started in television. Acting much more confident than he felt, Regis strolled into Flanagan's office and told the assistant he was an old friend of the former marine. Although Regis looked barely old enough to vote, much less to be a crony of Flanagan, the ruse worked – until Flanagan came out and demanded to know exactly who Regis was. Regis admitted he was just trying to get a job, and the program director promised to keep him in mind for any opening that might arise. Thinking that he'd finally taken the first step toward his career, Philbin headed back to New York to visit his family and eagerly await Flanagan's call.

His family members were thrilled to see him after his two years away, but they were less than enthusiastic about his career aspirations. Philbin's press agent uncle, Mike Boscia, felt compelled to burst his nephew's bubble by telling Regis that Flanagan would probably never call. But, not wanting Regis to be left hanging completely, Uncle Mike got him a job as an NBC page. His first assignment was as an usher for *The Tonight Show*, then starring Steve Allen.

Being able to see the top names of the day in person, even from the balcony seats, was a magical experience for Regis. And, as the weeks passed, his moment of seeming triumph in Flanagan's office began to fade – until the day Regis received a telegram from KCOP asking for his phone number. In his nervousness over barging into Flanagan's office, Regis had forgotten to write it down on his résumé. However, proving himself to be a man of his word, Flanagan had tracked Regis down using his address and offered him a job as a stagehand.

Ironically, now that the offer had come through, Regis was suddenly torn about what to do. Although Hollywood beckoned like a glittering muse, New York was his home. He had his family and his friends all around him, and he liked his job as a page. But when he took a step back from his own emotions, Regis knew California was the place to be for those interested in television. New York had neither the studio space nor the inclination to develop television as a major medium. "It was cheap and easy to make shows in Los Angeles," Philbin noted in his autobiography, *I'm Only One Man*. "New York was on the verge of losing billions and billions of tax dollars by allowing this burgeoning industry to slip away. Years earlier, the city had lost the movie business for the same reason. Now it was happening again." So in 1955 Regis packed his few belongings in a bag and flew to Los Angeles, checking in to a nondescript hotel near the station that would become his new home.

In the mid-1950s, most television shows were broadcast live, so working at a station was an exercise in keeping on one's toes. As a stagehand, Regis did a bit of everything, from driving a truck to holding the cue cards. Always hoping to get noticed, Regis thought it would be funny to write up anonymous tongue-in-cheek reviews of KCOP's programs and post them throughout the lot. Unfortunately, management wasn't amused, and when Flanagan found out Regis was behind the prank he gave him a severe verbal reprimand. He also gave him a promotion. In addition to his other duties, Regis became a fledgling newswriter for the station, producing copy for a newsman named Baxter Ward. When KCOP added a sports show to follow Ward's newscast, Regis picked up another assignment, this time as a researcher-writer-producer for the show. His most memorable moment occurred when the host, Tom Duggan, missed work and Regis was asked to fill in for him. Although he held his own, it was a one-shot deal, because Duggan never missed another day. But finally being on air was everything Regis thought it would be, and after that first taste it became his drug of choice.

But the strain of working three jobs began to undermine Regis's happiness. As much as he loved to work at KCOP, he also felt somewhat used and taken for granted. Resentment crept beneath his usual jovial exterior and ultimately led to a heated exchange with Flanagan, after which Regis left the station.

It's one thing to leave a job when you have another one lined up; it's quite another to walk out the door not knowing when you'll work again. That's especially true in the television business, because there's never a shortage of people willing to work long hours for low pay. Despite the experience he'd gained, Regis was unable to secure another job, and as the weeks passed he began to wonder if his dream had died a premature death.

In retrospect, though, Flanagan probably did Regis a favor by letting him go. He no doubt saw that Regis had ambitions far beyond what he could reasonably achieve at KCOP, and this would explain why Flanagan later called Regis and told him about a radio job in San Diego and wrote a letter of recommendation that helped to get him hired. Once again Regis was on the air, as a news reporter for KSON – though it wasn't exactly the stuff of high drama. He worked the morning shift, and San Diego in 1957 was one of the most peaceful, uneventful cities imaginable. The lack of crime and corruption forced Regis to do what he did best: improvise. He'd take the most unremarkable story and have fun with it, all the time honing a skill that would later inform his entire career.

San Diego was as much a new beginning personally as it was professionally. Not only was Regis trying to kick-start a career, but he was also trying to adjust to being married. He'd dated in high school and at college, but his relationship with Kay Faylen was his first serious romance, which resulted in a short courtship and a quick marriage. Kay's father was Frank Faylen, a well-known character actor who appeared in over 150 movies but was probably best known for his two television roles – as Dobie Gillis's father and as Herbert Bollinger on *That*

Girl. It's hard enough settling into a marriage under the best of circumstances, but Regis had chosen a profession rife with stress. After being let go from KCOP, he'd tread emotional water waiting for the phone to ring, unsure what the future held or if he even had a career anymore. The stress of his job, along with his and Kay's youth, would eventually create friction and begin to undermine the marriage.

But in those early days in San Diego, all seemed to be right with the world. Regis threw himself into his work and was buoyed by the positive responses his news reports generated among listeners, including some who worked at television stations. When KFMB-TV offered him a spot on the nightly news to present his Philbinesque news stories, Regis jumped at the chance to get back on television. A year later, another local San Diego station, KOGO-TV, channel 8, upped the ante and offered him an anchor spot on the 11 p.m. news and a feature spot on the 6 p.m. news. But the biggest carrot dangled in front of him was the possibility of hosting his own talk show at some point.

In 1961, Regis thought his career was finally coming together. KOGO-TV, channel 10, agreed to give him his own show, called *The Regis Philbin Show*, which aired every Saturday in the late-night slot. That year, Kay gave birth to their first child, a girl they named Amy. But his talk show was a strict mistress and took up the majority of his time, energy, and attention. His goal was to parlay this local coup into national exposure. Although he'd dreamed of this opportunity for years, now that he had the show he realized how much on-the-job training it would require. But it was through *The Regis Philbin Show* that he'd hone his unique style of "host chat," which would become his stock in trade.

Part of his style developed from sheer necessity. "We had no staff, literally," Philbin explained on the WCHS-TV8 web site. "No writers, no band even to sing a song with. I would just talk to the audience about what I did that week. I'd sit on a single stool and talk about whatever I saw or experienced that week, and that's how this whole dialogue began. It wasn't a monologue; it was a dialogue between me and the camera – and I guess it became a trialogue when co-hosts started joining me later."

"Back then," added Tom Battista, who worked with Philbin in San Diego and St. Louis, "anchors wrote eighty percent of their own copy. As talented as Regis is on his talk show, he is equally talented as a writer."

Years later, after being a talk show host had become second nature, Regis still called that first program, "The greatest talk show I ever had. I had no tools to fall back on," he pointed out to *Esquire*'s Bill Zehme in 1994. "I wasn't a comedian. I wasn't a singer. All I could do was what I did as a kid on the street corner . . . and I was a scream on the street corner!"

For three years, Regis regaled the audience and his guests with his slice-of-Philbin-life anecdotes. In those early years, what he lacked in experience he balanced with unbridled enthusiasm. Entertained by him or annoyed by him, everyone would have agreed he certainly seemed to enjoy what he was doing – whatever that was exactly. Not only did the program give Regis a forum in which to develop his broadcast skills, but it also became the conduit for one of his most enduring friendships. The show's stage manager was Tom Battista, who'd worked as the stage manager on Regis's 6 p.m. news report on channel 10. The two had hit it off, and when the talk show began Philbin had asked Tom to direct it. The two remain close friends to this day.

Slowly but surely *The Regis Philbin Show* edged its host closer to his ultimate goal: Hollywood. Regis signed with an agent in Los Angeles and waited impatiently for the phone to ring. Finally, the call came, and in October 1964 Regis thought he had his big break. Broadcasting giant Westinghouse wanted to replace Steve Allen in its nationally syndicated late-night talk show. Allen had become weary of the creative grind, but Westinghouse wanted to keep the franchise going, and, on the strength of some glowing reviews and the tenacity of his talent agency, Regis had become a viable alternative for Westinghouse – he was a fresh face and an apparent crowd pleaser.

But it would be tough to measure up to Steve Allen. Already in the early 1960s, he was considered one of television's pioneers. In 1954, he was the first host of *The Tonight Show*, originally just called *Tonight!* He followed it with a prime-time variety show, *The Steve Allen Show*, which aired opposite *The Ed Sullivan Show*. After a brief, unsuccessful stint on *The New Steve Allen Show* for ABC, Allen was hired by Westinghouse to host a 90-minute talk show, which in many television markets was aired opposite *The Tonight Show*, which now starred Johnny Carson. So not only was Regis being asked to take over from Allen, but he was also supposed to do so opposite Carson.

All the anxiety Regis felt after scoring the professional coup of succeeding Allen turned into a personal nightmare worse than he could have imagined. In San Diego, Regis had become accustomed to a largely improvisational style in which he chatted about what had happened in the world – primarily *his* world – that day. This seemingly simple stream-of-consciousness patter was actually part performance art and part comic monologue. However, because of his "gee whiz" delivery, its cleverness was masked. So often, even though people liked Regis, they couldn't figure out why. But the new show was run on a two-week tape delay, so whatever happened on a given day would be old news by the time the show aired. The style Regis had spent years honing was suddenly useless. It was a typical Hollywood marriage between producer and personality – "We love you, let's hire you, now let's change you."

"What could I possibly talk about that would have relevance two weeks from now?" Regis rhetorically asked Jess Cagle of *Entertainment Weekly* in 1992. "I have to be live, and be able to relate something that has happened in my real life. I don't know how to use writers. I remember being in a hotel suite in San Francisco before the show premiered and staying up until dawn, literally in shock and scared to death."

Philbin also struggled with the way Westinghouse managed every element of the show. In San Diego, he'd had no writing staff and had booked his own guests. At his new job, writers were assigned to him, mostly to write filler patter and jokes – which resulted in Regis looking stiff and sounding stilted. "I had never told a joke in my life," he said in *I'm Only One Man*. Equally bothersome was that decision making about guests was also taken out of his hands. So, when the show finally made its debut with Regis in the host's chair, he felt like an out-of-body observer, and the obvious lack of chemistry between him and the audience created a palpable vacuum. Not even the Terry Gibbs Sextet, a noted jazz combo who'd backed up singers such as Dinah Washington, could supply the missing energy.

To the surprise of many within the industry, the awkward show was renewed after the first 13-week run for another 13 weeks. In retrospect, perhaps it would have been less cruel had Westinghouse just pulled the plug rather than give Regis hope the show was going to make it, because shortly after granting the renewal Westinghouse told Regis he was finished. He was being replaced by Merv Griffin. Just like that Regis went from the next big thing on the small screen to the latest Hollywood afterthought. During the interview with Cagle, Philbin said of this time, "I psychologically was not ready for it. So I failed miserably." Being let go was emotionally devastating for Philbin; it was "one of the worst days of my life. The first time is always a shock. After that it gets easier."

In the mid-1960s, cable was a far-off broadband dream, and the term "weblet" had yet to be invented. And, with only three television networks, talk shows were rare, so there weren't a lot of options for Regis. After some nerve-wracking months of unemployment, he eventually found work on two weekly television shows. The first was a Saturday-night program airing on KFMB in San Diego, where he still lived. The other was a weekday show airing on Los Angeles's independent station, KTTV, to which Regis commuted. He was one of five hosts employed by the station; the others were Louis Lomax, Melvin Belli, Tom Duggan (whom Regis had worked with years before at KCOP), and Joe Pyne. Of the five hosts, Pyne was probably the most notorious and termed his brand of talk show "fist in the mouth," a precursor of the shows of Morton Downey Jr. and Jerry Springer. The Don Rickles of hosts, Pyne would insult not only his guests but audience members as well. His specialty was controversy, whether it was to invite a member of the American Nazi party onto the show or to quiz Lee Harvey Oswald's mother about her son. Regis was the antithesis of controversial. He modeled himself more after Jack Paar, hoping to establish an early rapport with the audience by spending the first few minutes of each show just chatting about his week.

What nobody could have guessed watching the outwardly cheerful Philbin was that, though he was gainfully employed again, he hadn't truly recovered from the failure of the Westinghouse show. And compounding that misery were the difficulties of raising a disabled child and the strain of trying to hold together a floundering marriage. In 1966, shortly after Regis had been fired by Westinghouse, Kay gave birth to their second child, a son they named Daniel, but his arrival was less than the joyous occasion they expected. Doctors at Los Angeles's Cedars of Lebanon Hospital informed the Philbins that Danny had been born with malformed legs – they lacked muscle tissue, he had no sacrum, and his lower vertebrae were fused. In other words, their son would never walk. Over the years, Danny would undergo over 60 surgeries related to his birth defect, and after one procedure he developed gangrene, which necessitated the amputation of one leg. Later his other leg would also be amputated, and attempts to use artificial limbs would fail.

Regis, always athletically active, would never be able to play an impromptu game of football with his son or challenge him to a game of tennis. As he says in his autobiography, he and Kay "could barely fathom it. My knees buckled. A wrench dug deep into my heart and it has stayed there ever since. I felt profoundly sorry and frustrated and angry." Although Regis tried everything from specialists to faith healers to cure his son, he eventually pulled away emotionally, unable to deal with the good intentions of friends that in fact made him constantly relive his agony over his son's condition. "I couldn't talk about it anymore. I suppose I should have handled it better; kept a stiff upper lip and smiled my way through the pain, like some people can. But I couldn't."

Adapting to the needs of a physically disabled child can cause even the best marriages to topple under the added stress. For Regis and Kay, it brought their marriage to the brink and would eventually push it over for good. However, marriages seldom end abruptly, and they struggled to stay together despite their increasing unhappiness.

Perhaps acting as a temporary salve was Regis's unexpected chance to get back onto the national TV stage.

Regis, Johnny Mann, and Joey Bishop, 1969

2

Regis the Sidekick

If Philbin lore is to be believed, Regis's stint as Joey Bishop's sidekick on the rat-packer's late-night talk show came about after a show Regis conducted on KTTV dealing with psychic healing. Philbin remembers that his agent, Noel Rubuloff, called to tell him the town was abuzz with the show – and, by the way, Joey Bishop was looking for an announcer-cum-sidekick.

Actually, this was hardly breaking news. ABC was hoping Bishop would give Johnny Carson's *The Tonight Show* its first serious competition. Ironically, Bishop had earned the opportunity to host his own late-night talk show after catching ABC's attention by being one of Johnny's substitute hosts. But even then *The Tonight Show* was considered *the* show to beat, and there was a big financial incentive to do so – in 1968, *The Tonight Show* would garner over $26 million in advertising, with sponsors paying $17,550 a minute for spots.

And to think that, back in the early days of television, late-night shows of any kind were a radical concept. The first show that tried to lure viewers in the later hours was NBC's *Broadway Open House*, really more of a variety show with comic Jerry Lester offering up singing, dancing, skits, and chitchat. The show was cancelled after 15 months, but it proved to NBC executive Sylvester "Pat" Weaver that late-night programming was viable. Three years after *Broadway Open House* went off the air, *Tonight!* debuted on September 27, 1954, with Steve Allen as host. His announcer and sidekick was Gene Rayburn, who'd later go on to be the longtime host of *Match Game.* The band was led by Skitch Henderson, and Allen enjoyed interspersing musical acts such as Andy Williams among the wide variety of guests.

Although most viewers take the "typical" talk show set for granted – a desk with a couch next to it – that format was developed on *Tonight!*, as was the practice of offering guests "scale" – or union "minimum wage" – for their appearances. But some of the innovations that Allen developed and that worked well for him because of his unique talents were later phased out, such as writing songs on the spot using suggestions from the audience. Like David Letterman would do decades later, Allen also often did silly man-on-the-street bits that required quick comic wit and improvisation. For 90 minutes a night, six nights a week, Allen kept up this grueling creative pace, and, beginning in the summer of 1956, NBC doubled his duties by giving him a Sunday-night variety hour, hoping to put a dent in Ed Sullivan's ratings. Not even Allen could keep up that pace, so in 1956 Ernie Kovacs was enlisted to sub for him on Monday and Tuesday nights. But NBC was more interested in pumping up its prime-time ratings than in maintaining its late-night viewership, and it decided to sacrifice the latter for the former. The network wanted all of Allen's time, talent, and energy devoted to the Sunday-evening show, so on January 25, 1957, *Tonight!* broadcast for the final time.

A few days later, NBC went from the sublime to the doomed when it premiered *Tonight: America after Dark.* Essentially a news program with a heavy focus on entertainment events, this follow-up to *Tonight!* was obviously not what Americans wanted to watch as they lay in their beds. By July, the show had been

cancelled. Reverting to the "If it ain't broken, don't fix it" philosophy, NBC unveiled *The Jack Paar Tonight Show* on July 29,
1957. Although popular and successful, the program would
eventually become a victim of its host's moodiness and edgy
personality.

Prior to assuming the host's job, Paar dabbled in radio,
television, and film. "I started as a radio announcer when I was
16," he recalls. "I was once the youngest announcer in the country, except for Bert Parks, who was a couple of months younger.
I had a terrible speech impediment and stutter, but here I was
announcing *Swing and Sway with Sammy Kaye* and *Rhythmic
New Deal with Dick Stabile.* I used to announce all those dance
bands at night, and when I was about 20, in Cleveland on the
CBS radio station, I was announcing the Cleveland Symphony
with Artur Dodzinski. I didn't speak Italian, but they used to
write everything out phonetically for me. And I would read this
stuff and pull it off. I had a very good voice," he says, then
laughs. "Actually, I'm kind of affected."

Whereas Allen had brought a finely honed comedic mind
to his show, Paar brought a studied intelligence and frequent ill
temper to his. His sidekick, Hugh Downs, was a curious coun-
terpoint to Paar's mercurial tendencies. Downs was almost
genteel in his bearing and would later sit behind the desk on
Mondays as the unruffled fill-in host. But when Paar was at the
helm, viewers saw what would later be called his "conversation
and controversy" style of hosting. "It was like riding a bronco,"
Downs recalled to Bill Zehme of *Esquire* in 1997. "Every night,
you didn't know what was going to happen, and it always did."

Paar, however, was also responsible for one of the most enduring formats of talk shows. "He had this idea," Downs told
Zehme. "He'd call me over and I'd sit in the chair, and when
the first guest came in, I'd greet the guest along with him and
move down to the couch and keep moving down throughout
the night. That is still done, and nobody's improved on it."

With his coterie of regular guests, which included Zsa Zsa Gabor, Hans Conried, and Peggy Cass, Paar was easygoing and genial. When interviewing political figures, though, he occasionally became confrontational. But as the show went on, Paar became inexplicably moody and clearly troubled. He entered into well-publicized feuds with the likes of Ed Sullivan, Steve Allen, and Walter Winchell.

Some of his escalating emotions could be attributed to both the stresses of doing a nightly show and television's social climate at the time. "At first, *The Tonight Show* was live," Paar says. "We were an hour and 45 minutes, and we had two writers. I wanted it to be 11:30 at night. I wanted people to talk softly – the feeling of people in bed. I protested when the audio levels of commercials were raised. When tape became an option after a couple of years, the networks wanted to tape the shows early. I said 8:15 p.m. is as early as I'll do the show. The other guys began taping in the afternoon, which is something that I think caused a great cultural difference."

Then there was the never-ending quest for guests. "Just constantly booking people. Every night, when the show was over, and it went really well, and there was applause, and the theme music was on, you'd feel great. You'd sit down at your desk for a moment, having done an hour and 45 minutes of ad-libbing. And then the memos would come in, memos asking who's available for, like, next month."

Paar spoke publicly about leaving the show, and viewers got used to hearing his complaints. But in February 1960 he stunned viewers, network executives, and Downs alike by actually walking off the show. What prompted the fit of petulance was the censoring of a joke about a "water closet," an English term for bathroom. Broadcasting being what it was then, the NBC censor cut the entire story without informing Paar. The following night, February 11, Jack walked onto the stage, voiced his fury at NBC and his frustration at constantly being in the center of controversy, and bid the audience farewell.

"I told a scatological story," Paar acknowledged years later. "I'm not proud of it, but it's not obscene. It's a funny, funny story. As I've said, I could read it in church. Not on Sundays, but I could read it during choir practice on Wednesday. Now, we were editing things all the time. I'd edit myself once in a while. If I said *Jesus* meaning *geez*, I would edit, put in a beep. I did it all the time, to myself and others. But this guy at NBC did something different. He stopped the show and put on three minutes of news."

Paar says that, when he first complained to NBC executives, they were dismissive and called him thin-skinned. He recounts what transpired: "'The newspapers are saying I said something obscene. I will not put up with it. I'll tell you what we can do. You say that you saw it, and it's not obscene, and that I should forget it, right?' I told NBC, 'If you really feel that way, I'll show that portion tonight, and that will stop the talk. They'll know what I said, and they'll see it's not obscene.' NBC called me and said, 'Jack, it'll look like you're running the corporation, and we cannot allow that.' I said, 'Is that final? I cannot run it tonight, even though you say it's not obscene?' They said, 'No, Jack, you can't.' And that's when I decided to leave."

Paar left Downs to face the TV audience that night. Hugh was the only person Jack had warned about his intention to walk off the show, but the advance word didn't ease matters. "The surprise to me was that he left at the beginning of the show!" Downs told Zehme. "I'll tell you, it was probably the hottest spotlight I was ever in, before or since."

Paar says that, when he said good-bye to the audience that night, he truly believed his *Tonight Show* career was over. "When I was leaving the only thing I'd ever done that was really successful, I thought it was the end. Honest to God, there was no trick. I never did anything for effect that I can remember. When I walked off, that was the end."

Actually, it wasn't. A month later, Paar returned, though he'd decided to return shortly after walking off the show. "The press was all around the house," Paar remembers. "So my wife and I climbed over a fence at midnight, and this guy brought a private plane into the Westchester Airport and took us out of there. And on the plane I read a column by John Crosby, a great television writer with the *Herald Tribune*. He had kind of needled me and made me mad, saying, 'This guy's given up everything, and nobody will want him,' or something like that. And I said, 'By God, I'm going to come back just to make John Crosby mad.'"

But Paar's tenure would never recover from his moodiness. Paar left for good in March 1962 after he was the object of media criticism for taking a camera crew to Berlin and broadcasting what was considered to be an inappropriately militaristic segment in front of the newly erected Berlin Wall. This time, though, he gave advance notice he was leaving, which allowed for a send-off from many of the celebrities who'd sat on his couch.

Among talk show hosts, Paar was the most influential for Philbin, not so much in his demeanor or interviewing style as in the way he'd open the show by coming out, sitting on a stool, and talking with the audience. The essence of what Regis would later call "host chat" he'd learned from Paar.

After Paar's final exit from *The Jack Paar Tonight Show*, there was a five-month gap before a new permanent host took over because of previous contractual obligations. But when Johnny Carson officially took over as host October 1, 1962, it was the beginning of an era that television – late-night, prime-time, anytime – may never see again. Over his 31 years as host, he would host more total hours of television than anyone else.

Ironically, Carson had initially turned down NBC's late-night offer, believing that the life expectancy of such a job was short. But he'd reconsidered and eventually made the genre his own. Although he retained Skitch Henderson as the band leader, he replaced Hugh Downs with Ed McMahon as the announcer and sidekick. McMahon and Carson had a history together, Ed having been Johnny's announcer on the quiz show *Who Do You Trust?* for the previous five years. Johnny also hired his brother, Dick, to be the director. From the first night, when Johnny welcomed Rudy Vallee, Joan Crawford, Mel Brooks, and Tony Bennett, it was clear he had a vastly different agenda than Paar. Instead of instigating confrontations and edgy moments, Carson sought to put both his guests and the audience at ease. His goal was simply to entertain, and to have a good time in the process, and he did so better than anyone before or since.

From the time television made its first broadcast, it has been a monkey-see, monkey-do medium. The economic and popular success of *The Tonight Show* would spawn a string of wanna-bes hoping to topple Carson's late-night monopoly.

ABC debuted its first competitor in November 1964 with Les Crane as the host. The gimmick employed by ABC was to have Crane use a special "shotgun" microphone that allowed members of the audience to speak directly with the guests. The format looked a lot better on paper than in reality, and Crane was cancelled after only four months.

Next up for ABC was *Nightlife*, which featured a different weekly host. That format didn't work either. So the network brought back Les Crane, adding Nipsy Russell and the Elliott Lawrence Orchestra for viewers who wanted an alternative to *The Tonight Show*. Few did, though, and in November 1965 *Nightlife* was mercifully put down. But network executives were still obsessively committed to succeed in late-night TV. If they couldn't beat Johnny on their own, maybe they could get an edge by hiring someone Carson himself had groomed.

In the mid-1960s, Joey Bishop was truly a household name. Born Joseph Abraham Gottlieb on February 3, 1918, in the Bronx, Joey dropped out of high school to work in vaudeville and as a stand-up comedian. He changed his name to Bishop after joining with Morris Spector and Sammy Reisman to form the comedy troupe The Bishop Trio. There was no sentiment attached to the name change, just pragmatism. Supposedly, the switch occurred only after their driver refused to chauffeur them unless they adopted his surname as their stage name.

Although Bishop went on to become a successful comedian in his own right, his true fame lay in his membership with the Rat Pack, along with Frank Sinatra, Dean Martin, Sammy Davis Jr., and Peter Lawford. Bishop didn't have as forceful a personality as the others, but he was still integral to the Rat Pack. "I gave them all those lines, man!" he asserted to *Dallas Morning News* reporter Ed Bark in 1998. "Nobody could out-ad-lib me in good taste." Perhaps part of the distance was also caused by his personal life. Unlike the womanizing reputations of the others, Joey was happily married to Sylvia – as he still is – and was a lightweight drinker by comparison, telling Bark, "I never had a hard liquor drink in my life."

Ironically, even though he'd eventually guest-host *The Tonight Show* a record 207 times (both before and after hosting his own late-night show), Bishop retained a resentment toward Carson, which might explain why he was willing to go against him in late-night TV. His bitterness stemmed from a 1965 benefit at which Sinatra, Martin, and Davis performed in St. Louis for St. Dismas House. Bishop was sick and therefore unable to attend in his usual capacity as master of ceremonies, so Carson filled in for him. "I was in the hospital and I'll never forgive Johnny for saying that I hurt my back bowing to Sinatra," he groused to Bark. "He was way out of line. If he wanted to say that, he could have also said, 'Joey, get well.' Johnny didn't know his place that night."

So it was with enthusiasm and incentive to burn that Bishop agreed to host ABC's next venture into late-night TV. Because of his association with the Rat Pack and because of his experience hosting *The Tonight Show*, ABC thought Bishop could seriously compete with Carson. The format would be what was by then traditional, with Bishop doing some comedy of his own before introducing the guests, and of course there'd be the sidekick announcer. The all-important question was who'd be Bishop's Ed McMahon?

Although McMahon was generally viewed as second fiddle to Carson, Johnny knew the importance of their chemistry, which they'd developed earlier while working on *Who Do You Trust?* What some people mistook as McMahon's sycophancy was in fact camaraderie between the two made easy by Ed's lack of competition with Johnny. That willingness to shun the spotlight is an essential component of being a successful sidekick. The idea is to complement, not overshadow, the host.

This was especially true of Bishop, a quiet comedian. His reserved demeanor always played in sharp contrast to the theatrics of his Rat Pack buddies. "The secret of comedy," Joey told the *Dallas Morning News*, "is when the audience can't wait to hear what you're gonna say. I see them doing comedy now so loud. My conception of true comedy is to be overheard, not heard. That's what made the Rat Pack so great." Because of Bishop's low-key stage presence, ABC certainly didn't want to hire someone who'd be a scene stealer, which in retrospect makes the decision to hire Philbin rather curious.

Regis believes he was hired only because Bishop decided ultimately he was the one to hire, over the objections of his circle of advisers. It was unusual to hire someone used to running his own show, especially someone with a definite point of view about how a talk show should be run. Regis doesn't hesitate to point out in his autobiography that, during his Saturday-night gig at kogo in San Diego, Walter Winchell once wrote in his column that Philbin had "style, class, dignity" and that he was "the only late-show personality around, we believe, who matches Johnny Carson's way with a guest or a coast-to-coast crowd."

Regardless of others' doubts, Regis was confident he had the unique qualities of a sidekick; as he pointed out in 1998 to *Esquire's* Bill Zehme, "The point of a second banana is that he is there always, at his man's beck and call!" At the time, however, Regis was more discreet, saying to *Newsweek*, "I feel comfortable in show business and I like to think I'm what Joey needs." He added that, during the audition, "Joey was utterly charming and made me feel important."

Of course, the early days of any show are usually a love fest, when hopes are high and the potential limitless. Bishop sought to set himself apart from Carson by being someone with whom viewers could feel a kinship. "I think the guy at home can identify with me because I ask questions about the same way, usually stupid, that he would," the comedian joked before adding seriously, "I don't want to be the hit of the show. I don't fancy myself as an interviewer. If we get something running, I let it go."

The Joey Bishop Show debuted April 17, 1967, with Johnny Mann and His Merry Men providing the music. Bishop's guests that night were Danny Thomas and then California governor Ronald Reagan. Only the most devout Bishop fan would say it went well. According to reviews from the time, Joey seemed to be overly impressed with Reagan and let Thomas carry on about patriotism. In a big way, the opening set the overall tenor Bishop's show would take: an emphasis on issues, which Carson refused to focus on. Carson's philosophy was simple. "Our show is entertainment," Johnny told *Newsweek* in 1969. "It's not hard to do an in-depth interview. It *is* hard to do a comedy show. The night audience is looking for entertainment, not a discussion of Viet Nam or civil rights." Or, as Johnny would say many times over the course of the show, "You don't compete against the competition; you compete against yourself." Even though Bishop was issue oriented, there were still plenty of laughs to be had. He mentioned to Bark in 1998 the time Richard Nixon appeared on the show. "I knocked on the men's room door and asked Nixon, 'Can I please come pee with you?' He said, 'What?' I said, 'Well, years from now people will ask me how well I got to know you. And I'll say, "How well? We peed together!"' But he wouldn't let me in! He thought I was serious!"

Regis succeeded in sublimating his own ego and presenting himself as Bishop's personal cheerleader. However difficult that was, being part of the talk show opened new career doors for Philbin.

According to him, once in a moment of camaraderie, he admitted to Bishop that as a kid he'd always wanted to be crooner Bing Crosby, with the melodious voice and ultrahip demeanor. So when Crosby appeared on the show as a guest, Bishop told him, "It would be the biggest thrill of Regis's life if he could sing 'Pennies from Heaven' to you." Showing either extreme grace under pressure or overblown ego, Regis stood up and serenaded Crosby, who listened quietly. That would no doubt have been the end of Philbin's singing career had not some executive at Mercury Records decided that having Regis record an album was the natural next step. Never one to turn down an opportunity, he happily accepted the offer and subsequently recorded an LP of standards, including "Where or When," "The Best Thing You Ever Had," "A Kiss to Build a Dream On," "Before Your Time," "My Rockin' Chair," "The Glory of Love," and, of course, "Pennies from Heaven." In the liner notes, Bishop tells listeners that, "for a man his age, he sings great."

Looking at the album cover now, with a tux-clad Philbin snapping his fingers and holding his mike against a green background that screams Swingers, the impression is retro kitsch.

But at least one modern reviewer says the entertainment value stops there. Amazon.com reviewer Ricky Wright notes that *It's Time for Regis* is "one CD that you won't mind seeing end after twenty-six minutes." He goes on to say that Regis "tonelessly" negotiates "the likes of *Mame, Swanee,* and a combo of *Toot, Toot, Tootsie (Goodbye)* and *Baby Face* that comes off not so much like a medley as the musings of a man who can't remember which song he's supposed to be singing." Wright finishes by saying, "as for the absurdly schizoid production, a meld of rinky-tink tempos and half-hearted pop-country moves, let's just say that it represented a boldly over-the-top aesthetic stance in the year of the *White Album* and *Beggars Banquet*," albums by the Beatles and Rolling Stones respectively.

The next door Regis went through was that of acting. Actually, it isn't too surprising that Regis began to dabble in acting since part of his talk show chat was performance art. His first dip into the thespian pool was a bit part in *Get Smart*, a now classic sitcom developed as a spoof of the spy craze that had been ignited by the James Bond films. The creative brain trust behind the series was Mel Brooks and Buck Henry, who also wrote the show.

Ironically, ABC was the first network to express interest in the series until it saw the first script and insisted that Brooks and Henry give Max a dog and a mother. While Brooks added Fang, he refused to add a mother for Max, so ABC rejected the script, saying it wasn't funny. NBC then ordered a pilot on the condition that stand-up Don Adams replace Tom Poston as Maxwell Smart. By the time Regis appeared on the show, it was in its third season and had already left its pop cultural mark thanks to Smartisms such as "Would you believe…?"

Philbin appeared in an episode called *The Hot Line*, which aired March 23, 1968. In the show, the evil organization KAOS discovers the phone number of the chief's hotline. It impersonates the president and orders Max to take over CONTROL, the counterintelligence agency he works for. Max does and sends the chief undercover as a singing waiter. Regis had little more to do than walk on and mug to the camera, but it was enough of a thrill that he'd rarely turn down any role that came his way.

But the professional highs Philbin experienced in 1968 were tempered by some distinct lows. After years of struggling to make their marriage work, Kay and Regis split up for good in 1968. It wasn't an amicable divorce. Years later Kay was quoted as telling friends that Regis didn't do a lot for their kids after the divorce. "He always wanted everything to be perfect. We weren't, and he let us know it," the *Globe* reported in March 1996. That sentiment was echoed by Maria Richardson, Danny's teacher's aid at the Desert Hot Springs Elementary School from 1976 to 1978. "I never met a nicer, more decent kid, but Regis never came to visit Danny, rarely called, and didn't write." One particularly painful episode was Danny's "graduation" from grade six, which neither parent attended, Regis because he was involved with work and Kay because the administration turned her away when she showed up apparently intoxicated.

Regis would later develop a close relationship with his son, but in those early years after his divorce from Kay his contact with Amy and Danny was sporadic, not only because they lived in different cities but also because Regis was starting a new life. He'd fallen in love with Joey Bishop's executive secretary, Joy Senese, whom he'd eventually marry and with whom he'd start a new family. Bishop was pleased with the pairing. "She was always laughing," he recalled to Elizabeth Sporkin and Sue Carswell of *People.* "I was glad that Regis was finding some happiness."

However, during that second year on *The Joey Bishop Show*, Regis was too consumed by his job to think much about wedding plans. Although Bishop's show had annual billings of

$11 million, its ratings were low and showed no signs of increasing. Joey was proud of the money the show earned because he thought he had "a lot of things going against me. ABC generally has the weakest news show, so the people start off on either NBC or CBS," he commented to *Newsweek* in 1969. "Also, both Carson and Griffin can dip into their house stable of stars. They have more big names on their networks."

Nonetheless, low ratings make network executives unhappy. And unhappy executives tend to look for weak links, so it was inevitable that those who'd been displeased with hiring Philbin would point to him as one of the problems. He was just one area of concern, of course, but he thought he was being singled out, and it led to an incident that remains murky to this day. What is clear is that in July 1968 Regis walked out during the middle of a show, just as his hero, Jack Paar, had done. At the time, he claimed he was upset over hearing talk that some ABC executives wanted to fire him. "The show got off to a slow start and I began hearing from ABC execs and people around Bishop that maybe I was the reason," Philbin told Zehme in 1997. "So one night, while on the air, I explained to Joey that I didn't want to come between him and success and I walked off." Philbin has also said that Bishop privately suggested he walk off just to see what would happen. Almost 30 years later, Bishop told the *Dallas Morning News* that Regis had walked off primarily because of a salary dispute, which is why he considered him "an ingrate. In the Hebrew religion, ingrate is the worst," he said. "I once told an interviewer that Regis is terrific. He gives lots of hope to people who have no talent."

But back in 1968 Bishop only sang his announcer's praises. "Regis Philbin is like a son to me," he said to *Newsweek*, "one of the nicest persons I've ever met." And, after a week's absence, during which the network was flooded with letters from viewers demanding that Regis come back, he returned to the show. But he was disappointed that Bishop's only comment was

"Ladies and gentlemen, all's well that ends well. Here's Regis" when Philbin was reintroduced and back in the sidekick's chair.

But to Regis it didn't end well. Although the show served as his big break, he was very unhappy during his stint, constantly frustrated and humiliated by the show's star, whose jokes were often at his expense. Looking back, Regis told Zehme he considers the sidekick role "a relic of the talk-show business! Feeding him was my job," he says of his role with Bishop. "Every night, I had to come up with something different. Joey never knew what it would be. Didn't want to know! He would just counterpunch, his specialty. But if it didn't pay off or wasn't cute, it was my fault." Regis added, "You had to know your place. You couldn't be funnier than him. It was important to me that he get his laughs. On the other hand, the perception of me was that of an inconsequential, trivial kind of guy. It was a tightrope act."

The show itself was also living its own precarious existence. It was one thing to go head to head with Carson and fall short – network executives were merely looking for a piece of the profitable late-night pie – but the complexion of keeping a low-rated show on the air changed in 1969 when CBS entered the fray with *The Merv Griffin Show*.

As the talk show gods would have it, the same day Johnny Carson debuted as host of *The Tonight Show*, Merv Griffin began hosting an afternoon chat fest, also on NBC. But after 26 weeks NBC cancelled the show because of poor ratings. Griffin went back to work as a game show host and bided his time. Then two years later he produced his own talk show and syndicated it through Westinghouse. The show's easygoing manner caught the attention of CBS, which had been looking for its own late-night personality, so in 1969 Griffin signed on with CBS. He came aboard with no illusions that he was going to unseat Carson; his hope was to bring enough new viewers to CBS to make his show profitable and its ratings respectable. He was even humble when comparing himself to Bishop. "By wearing both hats," he said to *Newsweek*, meaning on-camera host and off-camera producer, "I gain a good perspective. Bishop is a performer. I'm just a broadcaster. So I try to be the best interviewer there is."

The Merv Griffin Show debuted on CBS on August 18, 1969, with the Mort Lindsey Orchestra providing the music and Arthur Treacher along as the announcer. Although the show would barely register a blip on Carson's screen, it would ultimately be the death knell for *The Joey Bishop Show*, which also found itself embroiled in a lawsuit when the Oakland Police Officers Association filed a $25-million defamation suit against Marlon Brando for remarks he made on *The Joey Bishop Show* about the shooting of a Black Panther. The suit was later dismissed, but the action emphasized that everything was starting to go wrong. Finally, on December 26, 1969, Bishop signed off – midshow. After his monologue, he told the audience he had an announcement to make. "I've had a good run here, it's been a lot of fun, and I've enjoyed it. But it's over. I'm going to go home and have dinner with my wife, and Regis is going to finish the show for me." And with that he left, never to return. Three days later, *The Dick Cavett Show* took over the time slot, but it too would fare poorly and eventually fade from the late-night horizon.

Nobody ever did find the right formula to rival Carson, and he would reign untouched until May 22, 1992, when he walked away without looking back.

Although unhappy that the show hadn't worked out better, Regis felt a sense of relief that it was over. The job had always been stressful, and in later years he'd remember it as one of the less enjoyable working experiences of his life. Plus he was in love and ready to meet new challenges.

Bishop, however, never seemed to recover completely and remained sensitive about perceptions, particularly of his abilities as a talk show host. Twenty-four years later, on November

22, 1993, he sent a letter to the *Los Angeles Times* in response to a blurb it had printed.

> I thought your item on late-night talk shows that included a mention of my show as a flop was a bit unfair. Less than a month after my show was canceled, the Carson show asked me if I would like to be guest host for a minimum of four weeks a year. I agreed and was the No. 1 substitute host in the '60s. Your chart covered the years 1983 to 1992. No one else who "flopped" in the '60s or '70s was mentioned, just me. It seems you put me in a category in which I do not really belong. In regard to the statement that I was mortified to see my "onetime sidekick Regis Philbin become a superstar," quite the opposite is true. I am very happy for his success and feel in some small way I may have helped him. I have not suffered any mortification whatsoever!
>
> Joey Bishop
> Newport Beach, California

Nonetheless, Bishop hasn't spoken to Philbin in years, and if asked about it Regis claims he has no idea why. But one thing he does know is that one should never underestimate the power of the stars. Prior to the Bishop show going off the air, noted astrologer Sydney Omarr was a guest on the last show and told Regis, "You're going to become a household name, a very famous name." Thrilled, Philbin asked Omarr how long that would take. The astrologer hesitated and then said somberly, "Twenty years." There were times Regis didn't know if he would survive that long.

Regis and his second wife, Joy

3

Job after Job

Regis Philbin faced the new decade of the 1970s with both hope and fear. The demise of *The Joey Bishop Show* meant Regis was again looking for steady work, especially important now that he was trying to start a new life with Joy, whom he'd married in March in a wedding chapel at Forest Lawn cemetery. At the same time, he was also trying to meet his obligations to Danny and Amy. However, the transition was difficult because the end of his marriage to Kay Faylen was anything but amicable. Although it's been reported that, as Kay's unhappiness in the marriage increased, so did her drinking, her biggest source of resentment stemmed from Regis's alleged emotional neglect of Amy and Danny after the divorce and the financial hardship of being a single mother with a disabled son.

Throughout his career, Regis has been reluctant to talk much about his marriage to Kay, which, he says, "didn't work or last." What he has said for the record is that "I was in my early twenties when I married my first wife. We did it hastily. The truth is, we probably didn't know each other well enough. That marriage was painful for both of us, even though it lasted eleven years and produced two terrific kids." He has also admitted in an interview with Larry Eisenberg in *Good Housekeeping* that "I wasn't ready. I wasn't mature enough to cope with everything that followed."

Kay Faylen now lives primarily in Waveland, Mississippi, and according to neighbors she is a "recluse who never socializes." She has never given an interview about her marriage to Philbin and even now will only concede, as she did to the *Globe* in January 2000, that "He finally achieved what he's been dreaming about his whole life – he's a household name."

Although Regis had been a household name to fans of *The Joey Bishop Show*, and the butt of some Carson jokes, he knew how quickly an audience can forget someone, and he soon slipped out of the national consciousness again as he waited to see which direction his career would take.

The good news was that he soon found himself working on two programs. The bad news was that one of them was in St. Louis. The Los Angeles-based show was called *Tempo*, a three-hour talk and information morning program on KHJ-TV, which paired Philbin with a couple of different hosts, including Ruta Lee and LA newsman Stan Bohrman. The same year, Regis began commuting to St. Louis from Los Angeles once a month for three years to host the CBS affiliate's *Regis Philbin's Saturday Night in St. Louis*, a variety show with almost vaudevillian overtones, such as sparring with wrestlers and sharing a mud bath with Betsy Palmer. As hokey as the concept may be now, at the time it was an audience pleaser and bettered *Saturday Night Live* in the local market. Both shows lasted three years and provided Philbin with a cross-country platform that kept him in the periphery of television viewers' consciousness.

In 1972, Regis also waded into big-screen waters when he appeared in the Woody Allen classic *Everything You Always Wanted to Know about Sex but Were Afraid to Ask*. The film was loosely based on Dr. David Rubin's best-selling book of the same name, comprised of vignettes that answer questions such as "Do aphrodisiacs work?" and a faux game show – What's My

Perversion? – featuring Regis as a celebrity panelist named Regis Philbin. Also appearing in the many cameo roles were Burt Reynolds, Gene Wilder, Tony Randall, Lynn Redgrave, and Lou Jacobi. But probably the sequence most remembered is Woody Allen's turn as a reluctant sperm. Damian Cannon of *Movie Reviews* notes, "The basis for this movie is a gem, picking up the most popular questions from a manual on sexual problems and creating fables around them. The script, by Woody Allen, is both endlessly inventive and extremely funny – for once Allen is able to branch away from his standard movie persona and showcase his wider talents. . . . One-liners are produced at a staggering rate; if one joke seems obscure you know that another will be along shortly. . . . Allowances have to be made for the movie's structure, which breaks everything up, and the individual stories enjoyed for what they are (some of these are so good that they could almost be expanded into films by themselves). Be prepared to laugh at other people's perversions [and] then wonder what Woody Allen would have done with yours!"

Joanna was born to Joy and Regis in 1973, but the year would be another trying one professionally for him. With two families to support, steady work was vital for him. But both *Tempo* and *Regis Philbin's Saturday Night in St. Louis* ended, and Philbin would be out of work for almost a full year.

Finally, in the summer of 1974, Al Flanagan, Regis's first TV boss, hired Regis to do sports on the Denver station Flanagan now managed. Then Philbin was hired as a temporary fill-in host for *A.M. Chicago* on WLS-TV, the ABC affiliate in the Chicago market. Regis was thrilled, and the audience response was so positive that he thought he'd be hired as the permanent host opposite Sandi Freeman. It would be especially good timing, for Joy was pregnant again.

The first inkling of trouble was when the station manager,

Lew Erlich, decided to try out one other person for the position,
Steve Edwards. Much to Philbin's dismay, once Erlich met
Edwards they realized they'd grown up in the same Bronx
neighborhood. Regis knew that this was potentially bad news.
So he wasn't completely surprised when word came down that
latecomer Edwards was hired, and Regis was left with a pregnant wife, baby daughter, and no job prospects. Although he
may not have been surprised, he was emotionally devastated,
and the constant setbacks were wearing him down. But he
couldn't feel sorry for himself too long or the business would
pass him by. So Regis tried to remain upbeat and prayed something would come his way. Fast.

In November 1974, Regis got a phone call from John C.
Severino, the general manager for KABC-TV in Los Angeles.
Severino had briefly crossed paths with Regis when Philbin was
subbing on *A.M. Chicago* and wanted him to do movie reviews
on the 11 p.m. news. His years of doing talk shows now paid
off handsomely. Because he had met so many actors as guests
either on his own shows or on *The Joey Bishop Show*, Regis was
able to get interviews with actors he otherwise might not have
been able to get. When the ratings on the late news began to
climb, Severino gave Regis a spot on the 6 p.m. news as well.
The hours were long – the two reports had to be different – but
Philbin thrived.

Ascribing to the "more is more" theory, when a host's position on *A.M. Los Angeles* suddenly opened up in 1975, Severino
hired Regis for the job, on the condition that he continue his
spots on both newscasts. Regis managed to keep up this killer
schedule for a year, until he physically couldn't do it anymore.
Finally, Severino relented and took him off the late news so
he'd be fresh for his morning stint.

From the beginning, *A.M. Los Angeles* was like breathing familiar air to Regis, because he was allowed to use his old San Diego

format of "host chat" to open the show and engage the audience, both in the studio and at home. His primary concern was that, every time a new producer came in, the show's setup would remain the same. Inevitably, the new producer wanted to shorten or get rid of the beginning chitchat, but thanks to Severino Regis was allowed to keep his brand of hosting intact.

His first cohost on the show was Sarah Purcell, 44, an upbeat blonde who'd grown up in San Diego and shared a similar background to that of Regis. She worked for KFMB-TV as a weather reporter before joining Regis on the *A.M. Los Angeles* show. A few years down the road, Purcell would become nationally known as one of the hosts of *Real People*, which ran on NBC from 1979 to 1984. But during her time on *A.M. Los Angeles*, she was a nice complement to Regis, a pleasant personality who seemed to enjoy his commentary. The only thing Philbin insisted on was that there be no talking prior to the show so that what the audience saw would be spontaneous. Despite their apparent ease with each other, if there was a downside to the Regis-Sarah pairing, it was that he could overtake the show with his loud, sometimes overexcitable, shtick, for Purcell didn't have a particularly strong personality.

It was during Regis's time on *A.M. Los Angeles* that Joy began dabbling in television herself, filling in as a substitute host. Regis enjoyed having her there, and their husband-wife chemistry seemed to tickle the audience. But when Purcell decided to leave the show to pursue some prime-time opportunities, Severino didn't consider Joy for the full-time cohost. Instead, he surprised Regis by hiring Cyndy Garvey, then the wife of Dodger star Steve Garvey. Regis wasn't particularly enthused with the idea. In his autobiography, he recalls telling Severino, "Isn't the co-host job a bit much for her?" The general manager then told Regis, "You're going to be the major co-host, and she's going to be the minor co-host." Regis noted wryly, "The only problem was, he never told her."

Garvey was more aggressive than Purcell when it came to expressing an opinion or drawing attention to herself. A pretty blonde, she challenged Philbin more often, and though it was a different kind of chemistry the pairing still worked. When he first joined *A.M. Los Angeles*, the show had dismal ratings, but by the time Garvey was entrenched as cohost the program had been propelled to the top of the local ratings heap. Despite his success in Los Angeles, Regis yearned for a national platform that would bring him the professional respect he still thought he was being denied. While hosting *A.M. Los Angeles* by day, he continued to pick up extra work at night, all the while looking for the national break that would propel him over the career hump.

In 1975, Regis hosted *The Neighbors*, a somewhat mean-spirited show that had five neighbors revealing gossip about each other for the chance to win prizes. Think *To Tell the Truth* meets *Jerry Springer*. Audiences then had less tolerance for or interest in the public humiliation of others, and the show lasted only a few months.

Then, a year later, Regis signed on as an on-the-field correspondent for another ABC effort, *Almost Anything Goes*, a game show based on a British series called *It's a Knockout*. In the U.S. version, three teams selected from various small towns competed against each other in outrageous stunts that included bizarre obstacle courses, pie-throwing contests, and swing relays, and each episode was filmed on location at one of the competing towns. In an ironic twist, on this Philbin-hosted game show, the winning teams didn't drown in cash or gifts; the prize was civic pride and the chance to be on national television.

Despite his desire to be respected by his peers, Regis himself perpetuated a less than serious image with some of his curious career choices, particularly when it came to films. In 1977, he appeared in *SST Death Flight*, also known in other incarnations as *Flight of the Maiden* and *SST: Disaster in the Sky*. However titled, it was one of the many cheesy, made-for-TV disaster flicks on the airwaves in the late 1970s. In the movie, on the maiden flight of America's first supersonic transport plane, the crew's fate hangs in the balance after a disgruntled worker sabotages the flight. And, if that isn't enough, there may also be a deadly flu onboard.

The common thread in all 1970s disaster movies was the "all-star" cast. In this movie, there was Doug (*The Virginian*) McClure hoping to get lucky with Tina (*Gilligan's Island*) Louise, Billy (*Soap*) Crystal onboard as a steward, Bert (*Tattletales*) Convey wondering what to do with his pregnant girlfriend, and Peter (*Mission Impossible*) Graves longing for a former love. There was also Regis playing Harry Carter, an annoying television reporter.

Also in 1977, Philbin appeared in the telefilm *Mad Bull*, a dramatic piece starring former football star Alex Karras as a successful but bitter professional wrestler who begins to have a new outlook after falling for a unique woman, played by Susan Anspach. A year later, Regis was in a strange Mae West film, *Sextette*, in which he played himself, while the likes of Timothy Dalton, Tony Curtis, George Hamilton, and Ringo Starr oohed and ahhed after West. Leonard Maltin noted, "Astonishing is the only word for this comedy about a Hollywood glamour queen whose many ex-husbands keep popping up during her latest honeymoon. Naturally there's curiosity value in seeing octogenarian Mae still strutting her stuff, but it wears out pretty fast." As far as a rating, Maltin summed it up in one word: "BOMB."

The Bad News Bears Go to Japan managed to kill off the once-successful franchise after it was released in 1978. In this third and final installment, Tony Curtis – a 1970s fashion plate to the extreme – takes the team across the Pacific to play a champion Japanese team, and Philbin plays a Philbinesque character named Harry Hahm. Somewhere from the first film to this one, all the charm was lost. On paper, it probably looked like a sure bet, but it ended up being yet another flop.

But while his film career, if one could call it that, sputtered and only reaffirmed Philbin's image as a celebrity wanna-be among his detractors, *A.M. Los Angeles* showed no signs of losing its grip on the ratings. Regis may not have been more than a big-screen bit player in Hollywood, but in morning television he was a king, and his perky, all-American cohost was a princess. However, as viewers would find out later, Cyndy Garvey wasn't living the fairy-tale life she exuded on the air. Her married life with Steve Garvey would eventually unravel and be played out in public, though this time Regis would be spared having to deal with it. Little could he imagine that a few years later another cohost's private life would become headline news.

Cyndy Garvey was born Cynthia Truhan in Detroit. Her father was in the air force and, according to Cyndy, was a brute who regularly abused his three children. "I can remember him holding me by the neck and hitting me, hard: that was when I made serious mistakes like shouting to my brother in the house or coming home from school with my shirt outside my skirt," *People* magazine quoted her in August 1989 in a review of her autobiography *The Secret Life of Cyndy Garvey*.

Although Cyndy was accepted at Vassar, financial constraints led her to attend Michigan State University in East Lansing. But instead of pursuing a career in medicine, she met and fell in love with Steve Garvey and later married him. As Garvey's status as a star on the Dodgers rose, so did Cyndy's profile. Her intelligence, quick wit, and blonde, California-girl looks and his square-jawed jockness made Steve and Cyndy the perfect LA couple, and Severino knew what he was doing when he hired her. What he didn't know was that her private life was unraveling. Nor did anyone else, because she was expert at keeping her private turmoil hidden. The only indication looking back is that some of her sparring with Regis carried an edge, and as time went on her smile carried shades of brittleness. In 1981, to the surprise of viewers, Steve and Cyndy Garvey separated.

While Cyndy was making host chat with Regis, inside she was seething. She would later reveal to *Redbook* writer Joan Ryan that, "On the exterior, I had a famous husband, two beautiful daughters, a lovely home – who are you going to whine to? I knew at 22 that I should leave, but it took me until I was 32 to realize that I was dying inside. Then I broke my silence and got out. But I could. I had a college degree and I'd always worked. I felt saddest for the many wives who didn't finish their educations so they could give their full support to their husbands' careers. They never developed a career path of their own. They were dependent and hooked on the lifestyle – and they were risking injury, even death." Cyndy also admitted in her autobiography that one day she went snooping in her husband's office and discovered what she said was a date book that detailed Steve's rendezvous with his secretary. Enraged, Cyndy found a bat and started swinging. "First the pictures of Steve on the wall. They cracked. Then the trophies on the shelf. They crashed to the floor. I was doing damage, lots of damage," she told Curtis Rist of *People* in March 1996.

Unlike Regis's future cohost, Kathie Lee Gifford, Cyndy never made her private troubles fodder for host chat. Maybe she should have. Years later, long after she and Regis had parted ways, she was still raging from the bitterness she felt toward her ex-husband and lashing out at seemingly anyone in her path. Eventually, her accusations that Steve had been a womanizer were proven. Just prior to his second marriage in early 1989, he faced a public relations nightmare when one girlfriend gave birth to a daughter and yet another announced her pregnancy.

But Cyndy still couldn't let go. In 1996, she was charged with five counts of filing false reports. She had claimed she was being harassed, but the authorities discovered it was Cyndy, now going by the name Cynthia Truhan, who'd been doing the harassing. During questioning, she broke down and admitted she had fabricated evidence and was in fact harassing her ex-boyfriend, restaurateur Hans Rockenwagner, 35. "You guys can do what you want," *People* reported she told police. "I don't want to go to court. I'd rather just go to some good counseling. I know what I've done. I went through a period of anger."

Cyndy also claimed to suffer from a "major clinical depression." In October 1995, she apparently attempted suicide and was rushed to a hospital after Rockenwagner found her and called 911. "Depression," she noted in a statement to the press, "can rob its victims of all sense of reason."

Sometimes Regis no doubt wondered if television executives had any sense of reason. By 1981, *A.M. Los Angeles*'s ratings in the nation's second-largest television market were well noted by syndicators, always on the lookout for local shows that could play nationally. No doubt the biggest syndication story would occur in 1986, when Oprah Winfrey went from being a Chicago mainstay to an American phenomenon. But syndicators were more leery of Regis, he claims, mostly because of his insistence that the show open with his patented host chat. "They never understood the simple magic of that opening segment – two people just talking," he says in his autobiography. "National audiences would never accept it, they said. But I was getting eager to try."

Philbin would soon get his chance. In 1981, John Severino was promoted to president of ABC and transferred to New York, just as Regis's contract was due to expire. Whether it was an oversight or not, Severino didn't commit Philbin to a new contract before his departure from KABC, so, when NBC chief Grant Tinker offered Regis a national network morning show, he didn't hesitate, believing this was the golden opportunity he'd been waiting for. But perhaps he was too anxious to spread transcontinental wings.

If there's one constant in television, it's change. What works this season may bomb the next, so timing is critical. Hollywood annals are full of series that might have been a particular generation's *Seinfeld* had they aired on a different day or premiered a few months later or earlier. When Philbin jumped ABC's ship to join Tinker and NBC, he didn't note that NBC had been struggling in the day part, as a network's morning and afternoon schedules are called. The culprit was David Letterman, who hosted a daytime show called – what else? – *The David Letterman Show*. From reviews and collective memories, it was a ratings disaster. Ironically, the show won two Emmys and was much the same show that would make *Late Night with David Letterman* such a hit. But the day audience is a completely different demographic than the late-night one, and that audience wasn't amused by Letterman's antics. Affiliates dropped the show as if *it* carried a deadly flu, and NBC's day ratings took a sharp hit.

This was the mess into which Philbin walked so blithely. As a result of their experience with Letterman, only a little over half of the NBC affiliates agreed to carry *The Regis Philbin Show*, so it was a goner almost before it aired – especially after Regis was informed that, by the way, the show would be only half an hour long. His host chat took over half that long, so it would be a quick hello and good-bye with his guest. Even more troubling was the taping schedule. To broadcast the show at 9 a.m. on the East Coast, Regis would have to tape the show the day before. Visions of his disaster with Westinghouse flitted in his now pounding head, but Philbin was still determined to give the show his best try.

But he would do so without Cyndy Garvey. By this time, she'd moved to New York, no doubt trying to get as far away as possible from her domestic problems. So Regis looked around and for a while had different celebrity guest hosts sit opposite him until he decided to approach Mary Hart about being his cohost. Hart, who'd later become the doyenne of *Entertainment*

Tonight, was making a name for herself locally on the news strip *P.M. Magazine* and exuded an upbeat intelligence Regis liked. Hart had been a Miss America runner-up in 1971 and had started out learning the talk show ropes in places such as Cedar Rapids, Iowa, and Oklahoma City, Oklahoma, but she was poised and confident on camera and had some heavyweight role models. "I've always looked to Barbara Walters and Johnny Carson stylistically, and I've always admired the ease of Walter Cronkite," she once said to *Entertainment Tonight*'s Lisa Schwarzbaum.

But no amount of aspiration would save *The Regis Philbin Show*, and it probably wouldn't have mattered if Regis had secured Liz Taylor to be his cohost. Not only did he have little affiliate support, but his old boss, John Severino, was also doing his part to ensure Philbin's demise for his perceived disloyalty to ABC. When Regis's show debuted in November 1981, ABC launched a full-scale promotional blitz on behalf of *A.M. Los Angeles*. Between that and the low number of markets watching Philbin's show, it died a quick but humiliating death after just four months. In a bit of irony, the show received an Emmy as Outstanding Daytime Variety Series, beating such competition as the popular *Merv Griffin Show*. But by that time Regis was already looking for work. Again.

One of his old producers on *A.M. Los Angeles* tipped him off that a new cable network called Cable Health Network was looking for shows. In cable's infancy, finding programming and talent was a constant battle, for many people were wary of being associated with the fledgling technology. But Regis couldn't afford to be picky, so he developed a show for the network, which later changed its name to Lifetime. *Regis Philbin's Health Styles* featured segments on health, fitness, and cooking, all presented in his now inimitable style.

But behind his can-do TV persona was a man going through a midlife career crisis. After taping the first order of shows, Regis sat around his house all day, waiting in vain for the phone to ring. Although Lifetime would pick up his show (it would run through 1988 and become the highest-rated program in the history of Lifetime), he was still lamenting his lost opportunity at national syndication.

In January 1983, the call finally came. An agent in New York suggested that Regis consider bringing his morning show expertise to New York. The ABC affiliate there, WABC-TV, was in a ratings tailspin, and Philbin was a proven daytime winner. The catch? The only person who could approve his hiring was John Severino, who'd made it clear he'd felt betrayed by Regis for going to NBC. But Philbin was desperate and had no choice but to call Severino, career hat in hand, and ask for a job. Although Severino agreed, Regis later had second thoughts about uprooting his family and at one point decided he couldn't do it. Only after he was offered the option of quitting after one year did he change his mind and agree to take over *The Morning Show*.

Regis was thrilled to be back home in New York and looked at his new job as a chance to start over, with a little help from the past. His first order of business was securing a cohost, and he immediately called Cyndy Garvey, who accepted. Considering how far in the ratings cellar *The Morning Show* was, Regis knew he could only improve the show's standing, and he did. The New York audience warmed to him and Cyndy just as LA viewers had. The program was pleasant and fun, and management was pleased.

Then in 1985 Garvey left to wage war with her personal demons, leaving Regis with a cohost chair to fill. The woman who'd take over for Garvey would also bring fun and enjoyment to *The Morning Show*. But the combination of Regis Philbin and Kathie Lee Gifford would also create ratings magic never before seen. Regis would not only meet his professional match but also stumble upon the secret combination for the success he'd stopped believing he'd ever find.

4

The New Cohost

Forget the old saying "Behind every successful man there is a woman"; in Regis Philbin's case, the woman most responsible for his current success started sitting *beside* Regis in 1985. After two years on *The Morning Show*, Cyndy Garvey decided to move on, and once again Regis was left with the task of finding someone new to sit in the cohost's chair. For a while, Joy filled the seat, but only as a stopgap measure. Then Ann Abernathy got a tryout, but it didn't last long. Looked at without the benefit of hindsight, Kathie Lee Gifford wasn't an obvious choice. But there's a lot about Kathie Lee that's not obvious at first.

Kathie Lee Epstein was born on August 16, 1953. Although raised in Bowie, Maryland, she was born in Paris, France, because that's where her father, Aaron, a chief petty officer in the navy, was posted. Kathie Lee would later tell Jeannie Park and Maria Eftimiades of *People*, "I knew from the day I was born I was loved." The first clue was when her father and her mother, Joan, sent out birth announcements that shouted "A Star Is Born." Little did they know how right they were; her mother remembers little Kathie Lee running around the house singing into a play microphone. But musical ability ran in the family – Kathie Lee's baby sister, Michelle, is a singer. So did religion.

Her father converted from Judaism to Christianity, her mother was a devout Christian, her older brother, David, is a minister, and when she was 12 Kathie Lee was saved while watching Billy Graham on television and became a born-again Christian.

In her autobiography, *I Can't Believe I Said That!*, Kathie Lee recalls the night of her spiritual awakening. "It was astonishing. Mom had switched TV channels and tuned in to a Billy Graham crusade. . . . I felt a mixture of awe and apprehension. Mom had been watching television alone and had spontaneously knelt down in front of the TV set, asking Jesus to be the Lord and Savior of her life. . . . Michie, having heard Mom weeping, was now kneeling and asking the Lord to come into her heart. The Christian faith was now a family affair. . . . Our minds were blown; we were about to be reborn." Prior to this evening, Kathie Lee says her family wasn't "particularly religious. . . . Though we respected my father's heritage, we were not practicing Jews, either. Because he and his father had been estranged, he had not been raised as an observant Jew but rather in his mother's Christian faith."

So, while many in her generation were embroiled in America's cultural revolution, Kathie Lee was still living a 1950s existence of sorts. Instead of zoning out on pot, she stayed home doing needlepoint. Rather than singing antiwar songs or crooning about free love, she performed folk songs with her sister at all-American places such as the Veterans Administration. She sang with a group called the Pennsylvania Next Right. So it was perfectly in keeping that she enter something as quaint and traditional as the Junior Miss pageant, especially since, even as a teenager, Kathie Lee wanted to be in the public eye in whatever way possible. In 1971, during her senior year of high school, she was Maryland's Junior Miss winner and received a $1,000 scholarship and the chance to compete for the national title.

However, any dreams she may have had for further winnings and exposure were dashed when she was thrown out of the national contest for breaking pageant rules – specifically, talking to a boy. She did get to meet one of the pageant's judges, though, Anita Bryant, who'd help to change the course of Kathie Lee's life.

In the early 1970s, Bryant, a former beauty queen herself, was a well-known singer and the ubiquitous spokeswoman for Florida Orange Juice. She was also an openly devout Christian whom Kathie Lee considered a hero and role model. After Bryant met Kathie Lee, she immediately took the young woman under her wing, because "she kind of reminded me of myself when I was younger," Bryant recalled to *People* in March 1994. "She was fun and bubbly." So, after Kathie Lee graduated from high school, Anita hired her to go to Key Biscayne, Florida, to work as her assistant and to occasionally watch her four children. Bryant also served as a personal mentor for Kathie Lee, offering spiritual guidance as well as practical assistance, such as helping her get into Oral Roberts University, where she enrolled as a voice major on a full music scholarship, intent on forging a career in the blossoming field of Christian entertainment.

At the university, Kathie Lee was asked to be a member of Oral Roberts's World Action Singers, a group Roberts featured on his evangelical television show. Despite the obvious opportunities she was getting, she decided to leave the university. "They tried to cookie-cutter all of us," she told Elizabeth Gleick and Sue Carswell of *People*. "I wanted the diversity of life. God went to the trouble to make us unique. They wanted us to believe the same way, think the same way." So Kathie Lee quit college shy of graduation to pursue her dreams of being her own kind of star, and this action caused her and Anita's paths to diverge widely.

A few years after working for Anita, Kathie Lee was shocked and dismayed when Bryant used her Save Our Children group to spearhead an effort to have an antidiscriminatory law against gays repealed in Dade County, where she lived. She spoke at rallies, calling it "ungodly" to protect homosexuals from discrimination, and even argued that the antidiscrimination law was a licence for homosexuals to recruit and molest children. Bryant also starred in a virulent, heavily funded television campaign spreading fear and ignorance. Her multipronged attack worked, and voters in Miami and Dade County went on to overturn the law by better than a 2-1 margin. Bryant tried to take her antigay message to other states, with decidedly less success, as gay groups and social libertarians were better prepared and countered with educational campaigns of their own. But many people look back and see Bryant's 1977 campaign as the beginning of the rise of the extreme right in America.

Although Bryant won the battle in Florida, in the end she not only lost the political war but also suffered professionally. Outraged at her media attack, some of the more flamboyant members of Miami's gay community took to the streets wearing T-shirts that said "Squeeze a Fruit for Anita." Her singing engagements and record deals dwindled to nothing. But the most damaging financial fallout was the loss of her contract as spokeswoman for the Florida Citrus Commission. Her personal life was faring no better. In 1980, her 20-year marriage to manager-husband Bob Green ended in a divorce, and Bryant was forced to leave Florida and start anew in her hometown of Tulsa, Oklahoma.

These days Bryant is remarried and performs in Branson, Missouri. She told *People* magazine that "people who come to my performances are hungry for the truth. They thank me for reminding them of the importance of God and country. I was patriotic back when patriotism wasn't in. I guess I was just a woman ahead of my time." Although she is mostly an entertainment footnote now, her name was recently in the news when in 1999 the repeal of the antidiscrimination act in Dade

County was overturned, making it a crime again for anyone to discriminate in housing, employment, credit and finance, and public accommodation because of one's sexual orientation. About her former mentor, Gifford has said many times in interviews, "She was very, very good to me," and she leaves it at that.

It wasn't the only time someone from Kathie Lee's past made far-right views a public matter. In 1999, it was reported that a former high school sweetheart at Bowie High School, Michael Bray, was now an infamous antiabortion activist who advocated violence, stating that killing doctors who perform abortions is "justifiable homicide." Bray, pastor of the Reformation Lutheran Church in Bowie, who has served four years for his role in bombing abortion clinics, told reporter Alan Smith that he still has a soft spot for Kathie Lee, his "childhood sweetheart. She was the cheerleader; I was the wrestler. We went to prom together and my fondest memory of her was her positive attitude. She was always upbeat, sparkling, happy." Kathie Lee and Bray drifted apart when he left to attend the naval academy and she kept her sights firmly focused on a career in music, and he faded into her past.

Unlike both her former mentor and her former beau, Kathie Lee tended to adopt a more open-minded spiritual policy, concerned more with one's own actions than with those of others. After dropping out of college, she remained in Tulsa and wrote a spiritual diary that chronicled what it was like growing up a born-again Christian in the Age of Aquarius. The book, *A Quiet Riot* by Kathie Epstein, would be published in 1976 by the Fleming H. Revell Company, which paid her $10,000 – a sum much needed and much appreciated by the aspiring performer.

In 1975, Kathie Lee moved to Los Angeles in search of a career and did the traditional circuit of young performers. She auditioned for countless commercials, was given hope by being cast in blink-and-you-miss-them roles in soap operas, including the usually mute Nurse Callahan for a year on *Days of Our Lives*, and worked on some gospel albums. Unlike other would-bes who spent their leisure hours in clubs or at bars hoping to meet someone who might help their careers, when Kathie Lee wasn't pounding the pavement, she spent time in a Bible study group. Which is why *People* writers Elizabeth Gleick and Sue Carswell report that she wryly says of her 22-year-old self at the time, "I was the Last Hollywood Virgin."

Not for long. One day at a recording studio in Hollywood, Kathie Lee met a handsome blond-haired, blue-eyed gospel composer and record producer named Paul Johnson, seven years her senior. She was in love, and the two would eventually marry in 1976. That much everyone can agree on. However, nearly everything else about her marriage to Johnson is up for debate, depending on whom you believe. According to Kathie Lee, even during the courtship Paul would waver between warmth and coolness, while she was feverish with passion and love. According to him, she was a borderline stalker. "She'd show up at my recording sessions and concerts and invite herself to parties at my house." When another producer asked Paul if he knew of any singers available for a Las Vegas gig, he recommended Kathie Lee "to get her out of my hair." But Johnson says his attitude changed after meeting her family and after they began spending more time together after her return from Las Vegas, and eventually he asked her to marry him.

As reported by Gleick and Carswell, in her autobiography Kathie Lee says that, when they got married, she was convinced she had made "the ultimate Christian catch." And she was anxious to shed her virginity for the fire of newlywed bliss. "It was, like, YABBA-DABBA-DOO! I lost every inhibition I'd ever had. It was time for candles and romance, time to boogie and swing from the chandeliers. And yet we just couldn't seem to get relaxed with each other." The marriage "was a real disappointment to me, as I know it was for Paul. We all want to love and be loved, and when it doesn't happen, it's devastating." Overall, their sexual intimacy was "not passionate, and it was not successful, but it was polite."

Professionally, however, things were heating up. Kathie Lee and Paul were gaining notoriety within gospel music circles, performing together and appearing together on the covers of Christian magazines. At the more secular end of show business, in 1977 Kathie Lee Johnson landed the gig of the "La-La Lady" on the syndicated music quiz show *$100,000 Name That Tune*. She was so named because she had to replace the actual words with la las so the contestants could guess the name of the song. In 1978, she was cast in *Hee Haw Honeys*, a spin-off of *Hee Haw*. Set at the Nashville restaurant Honey's Club, the syndicated corn pone starred Kenny Price and Lulu Roman as the owners with Kathie Lee and Misty Rowe playing the daughters who both waited tables and sang. The gimmick was to have a different country-and-western performer appear each week as the guest star and regale the audience with a song or two. Although the show only lasted until 1979, it offered Kathie Lee more exposure than she'd ever had before and led to her appearance in Las Vegas as the opening act for the likes of Bill Cosby and Bob Hope.

But for all her professional achievements, Kathie Lee claims her heart was being crushed daily because of her faltering marriage. She realizes now that her six-year marriage to Paul Johnson was "an illusion." Although they sought counseling from both secular therapists and from ministers, they were drifting irrevocably apart, even though Kathie Lee tried to maintain the romance. She says she came home one day in 1981 and discovered Paul had moved out. "When I was divorced, my foundation was ripped out from under me," she told Joanna Powell of *Redbook*. "I spent almost two years being very lost. I had always been a strong person, capable and confident, but divorce was devastating. When you've saved yourself your whole life to be a gift to a man who then basically returns the gift and says it's not for me, it's crushing. In the world I grew up in, divorce is not an option. You stay married, you work out your fights and battles, and you pray." However, she also says in retrospect that it was the best thing, personally and professionally, that could have happened.

Paul Johnson has a completely different recollection of their marriage, life together, and eventual split, and, after details of the marriage came out in Kathie Lee's autobiography, Johnson and others spoke up. "I have much different memories of my wedding night with Kathie Lee," he wrote to *People* in November 1992. "The honeymoon pictures I have show both of us to be happy and playful and very much in love. Everything about it was 'successful' for me. This is the first time I've heard that it wasn't for her. In spinning this yarn to have a best-selling book, Kathie Lee has documented to the world the very reason why our marriage failed. It's impossible to build genuine intimacy with someone who converts every private and sacred moment into burlesque material for her public forum."

A close friend of Johnson, Roy M. Carlisle, adds, "Kathie Lee Gifford has turned her need to rewrite history into a Judas-like fine art. I have known Paul Johnson, her first husband, like a brother for over twenty-four years, and I listened to his pain during the marriage and the divorce. We who were there know that Kathie Lee's version of the story will please her fans, but if it gets fact-checked at the pearly gates, she is in deep *caca*."

Paul was incensed enough that he decided the only way to fight Kathie Lee's national pulpit was to find a soapbox of his own. So in 1999 he broke his silence and gave an exclusive interview to Alan Smith of the *National Enquirer*. Johnson claims that, among other things, what broke them up was primarily Kathie Lee's blind and naked ambition. "We couldn't even watch a TV show without her saying, *I should have been that Charlie's Angel*. . . . Sometimes when Kathie Lee didn't get what she wanted, she would pout for days and punish everyone around her. Kathie Lee can pout louder than anyone I know. . . . It is exhausting living with someone so absorbed with themselves. Kathie Lee lives as if the cameras are rolling twenty-four hours a day. She's always *ready for her close-up*."

In the end, Johnson says, her career and her belief that he wasn't paying enough attention to her sparked the argument that finally broke them apart. According to him, it was Kathie Lee who asked for the separation while they were away in Hawaii. She flew home alone, and when he joined her later he told her he had to leave for his "sanity's sake." He also says that, after hearing his ex-wife talk about him and reading what she has written, he's come to the conclusion that "Kathie Lee never lets the truth get in the way of a good story."

After her divorce, Kathie Lee was perhaps a little on the outs with the Christian entertainment community. She is the first to admit that during this period she kissed her virginal ways goodbye. "Let's just say I was not the best little girl in the world anymore," she once told Elizabeth Gleick and Sue Carswell of *People*. She dated many men, but her experiences seemed to give her little joy. "I had no direction," she told *Redbook*'s Powell. "I was working and dating. I was in relationships that were destructive, trying to be loved because I'd been rejected. Maybe this person will love me; maybe that person will love me."

Whether in spite of or because of the crossroads she was at in her personal life, Kathie Lee's career was on a definite upswing. With her marriage having disintegrated, Kathie Lee signed to headline a series of Carnival Cruises commercials. Then she ended up in Manhattan after being hired by *Good Morning America* to do some field reports as one of the regular correspondents. She rented an Upper West Side apartment and was eventually promoted to filling in for *Good Morning America* host Joan Lunden. During one of her hosting stints, David Hartman was also on vacation, and his fill-in was former New York Giants halfback Frank Gifford. The two hit it off immediately, in part because of an unspoken empathy – Gifford and his wife, Astrid, were in the death throes of their relationship, an experience fresh in the mind and heart of Kathie Lee. But she insists they were strictly platonic friends in those early years. "He seemed so uninterested in me," she said to Elizabeth Sporkin and Sue Carswell. "I thought, 'What a wonderful guy,' but a serious relationship really never dawned on me."

At the time, Kathie Lee was also busy preparing to start a new job. When ABC asked her to sit next to Regis on the WABC morning show, she saw the position as just another stepping stone. She had no clue it would become her own personal career platform.

While on *Good Morning America*, her blurt-it-out style sometimes seemed to be inappropriate, but opposite Regis during the all-important host chat segment it played like commedia dell'arte. "My God, she is so alive!" Regis recalled thinking. "She makes David Hartman look like a young guy." In Philbin's amusing foreword to Kathie Lee's autobiography, which he titled "Where Would You Be without Me?," he recalls about their first meeting, "I had to shield my eyes."

But their disparate personalities, which have been frequently described as vinegar meets honey, captured the fancy of viewers. After having been a steady if not spectacular daytime program, *The Morning Show* suddenly saw its ratings soar, and within the first year Regis and Kathie Lee were hosting the top morning program in the New York market. And Regis was suddenly the apple of New Yorkers' eyes. In 1986, one *People* reader asked, "on behalf of the many thousands of Regis Philbin fans, I ask . . . why not Regis Philbin for a *People* cover story? Regis is the warmest, wittiest wise guy in the Big Apple. He has it all, charm, style, humor, sincerity. So . . . you can go to bed after Johnny Carson – we'll wake up with Regis!"

Suddenly, both Regis and Kathie Lee started popping up in the strangest places. He continued his penchant for appearing in box-office busts, so to speak, such as the 1985 flop *Malibu Express*, which featured four bare-breasted *Playboy* Playmates. Regis and Joy did cameo bits as – what else? – talk show hosts in the film, directed by Andy Sidaris, a friend of the Philbins. Regis was also dabbling in entrepreneurship, investing in the restaurant Columbus with, of all people, Mikhail Baryshnikov. But as Alan Richman's review for *People* indicated – the eatery got a no-stars rating – restaurant business can be as brutal as show business. "After hearing that a glimpse of Regis was practically a sure thing," Richman wrote, "I rushed over to Columbus for lunch. No Regis. 'He's on vacation,' I was told. I don't blame him. From food like this anyone would need a vacation. . . . We were seated at a plain, varnished table decorated with flowers so wilted that they might well have been thrown onstage the last time Baryshnikov danced. One of our luncheon entrees, chef's salad, consisted of lots of iceberg lettuce topped with lots of shredded carrots and garnished with stringy roast beef and a few chunks of cheese that the cook was too listless to slice all the way through. The other entree was a thick, dry, steamy omelet that tasted pre-made and microwaved, like airline breakfast food. Desserts were a spoiled strawberry tart with bitter yellow cream and Peach Melba made with canned peaches. . . . Columbus, a restaurant where hardly anybody goes to eat, is actually the premier late-night celebrity hangout on Manhattan's Upper West Side. While we were having lunch, Danny Aiello walked in, looked around and walked out. He's not only a fine actor, he's also a promising restaurant critic."

In July 1986, Kathie Lee's personal and professional lives converged, because that's when Kathie Lee says she fell in love with Frank Gifford, who'd been separated from Astrid for almost two years. Kathie Lee recalls that she used to cry on Frank's shoulder about her boyfriend troubles and that Frank would console her and offer advice until he finally decided he didn't want to be a sounding board anymore. She recalls that he said, "I'm not going to listen to this anymore. You're going to hang out with me." She also told Jeannie Park and Maria Eftimiades of *People* that she lost her heart to Frank at a party after he sang "You Don't Bring Me Flowers" with her. Apparently, Frank sang with "no rhythm, no tone, nothing. I fell off the sofa laughing. I looked at him and thought, 'I don't want to live without that man.' It's a wonderful thing to fall in love with your best friend." A month later, once her divorce was final, Kathie Lee says Frank proposed to her and presented her with a five-carat diamond engagement ring. They were married on October 18, 1986, amid accusations by Astrid that Kathie Lee and Frank had begun an affair prior to when they claimed, tacitly implying Kathie Lee was a home wrecker. And other members of Frank's family were troubled by the marriage, including his children, who were the same age as Kathie Lee, 23 years Frank's junior. She told *Redbook*'s Powell that Frank's sons seemed to accept her more readily than his daughter. "She's been the apple of his eye all her life so there was a natural holding back," Kathie Lee said. "Frank was wise and he said, 'Just give her time, she'll see that we really love each other.'"

For some, the lovey-dovey romance smacked more of a public put-on than a real relationship, but *The Morning Show* audience ate it up. Buoyed by the rabid loyalty Kathie Lee generated among her fans, ABC executives decided the Giffords would be a natural on-screen pairing that viewers across the board would embrace. So, when it came time for the network to air the 1988 Winter Olympics in Calgary, Kathie Lee and Frank were hired to host the network's late-night wrap-up show. It was an idea whose time had obviously *not* come.

"These Winter Olympics are the longest ever," wrote Steve

Wulf in *Sports Illustrated*. "But the Games must seem even longer to ABC's Frank and Kathie Lee Gifford, hosts of the network's late-night wrap-up show." Wulf commented about the "homey" set, which included a small library. "For those who might be curious, the books include *Hotel* by Arthur Hailey, *Rachel, The Rabbi's Wife* by Silvia Tennenbaum and seven – yes, seven – copies of *Blind Ambition* by John Dean."

Another *Sports Illustrated* writer, William Taaffe, gave his award for Worst Studio Show in an end-of-the-year review to the "Frank and Kathie Lee Gifford patter-and-drivel exercise during the Winter Olympics. The most memorable observation Kathie Lee had in two weeks was how healthy the Canadian farm babies looked. Or maybe it was her comment on Billy Kidd's cowboy clothes: 'I want that hat. It goes with my outfit!'"

But Kathie Lee seemed to be impervious to criticism. She would later say to Phil Rosenthal of the Los Angeles *Daily News* that, "If I had listened to one critic early in my career, I would never, never have shown my face in public again." So she adopted a hear-no-evil attitude that would see her through the most scathing reviews. What also helped the criticism to roll over her was that she and Regis were the undisputed queen and king of New York morning shows.

Finally, inevitably, Philbin and Gifford were approached by Buena Vista about syndicating the show nationally. Regis had been down this road before, twice, and knew that he probably wouldn't get a fourth chance. So he would agree to the syndication deal on one nonnegotiable condition. "I said, 'Leave the first seventeen minutes alone,'" he told *People*'s Sporkin and Carswell. "And they did." Which is not to say *Live! With Regis & Kathie Lee* would air live nationally; it would be aired live in the eastern time zone and on same-day tape delay in the rest of the country.

Philbin understood why host chat was worrisome to the un-initiated. "It's deceptive what we do," he explained to Rosenthal.

"I don't know anyone else who dares to go on television without knowing what the hell they're going to talk about." He'd later elaborate to Evonne Coutros of the *Record*, "There is no script to the show. It's all brute ad lib. So you're a little bit more anxious because you frankly don't know everything you're going to say or how it is going to come out, so there's that heightened risk that activates you. Naturally, you're pretty excited when doing the show, and I guess it shows. It's just the fact that you're live and walking on that tightrope."

Philbin was also faced with the question of whether his brand of show would play in the great American heartland. As he said at a press appearance at NATPE, "Are they going to understand you in Kansas City? Are they going to enjoy you in Cleveland? Those are the kinds of questions we ask."

Gifford saw another difficulty, telling UPI's Valerie Kuklenski that the challenge of host chat was "to do it in a way that only pokes fun at itself and doesn't create envy in another person. My mom and dad came from nothing, I've been one of those people. So, I try to tell a story without creating an aura of 'Don't you wish you had my life?' because that would be cruel." Ironically, that very criticism would dog Gifford throughout the ensuing years.

In 1989, *Live! With Regis & Kathie Lee* debuted to a national audience, and television viewers were instant converts, as were surprised television critics. *Entertainment Weekly*'s Ken Tucker noted in 1990 that the biggest drawback of daytime talk shows was their predictability. "*Live! With Regis & Kathie Lee*, however, is funny, energetic, and surprising." And Tucker wrote that the credit "must go to that feisty little pit bull of popular culture, Regis Philbin. . . . The opening segment of each day finds Philbin fulminating: against the movie he saw the previous night, against the music his daughters are listening to, against some story in the morning's newspaper – against, in short, anything and everything. But it's entertaining anger. He's laughing even as he works himself into a lather." And, with Kathie Lee added to the mix, Tucker viewed the coupling as "an agreeable mismatch: He's always needling her about her endlessly changing hair . . . [while] she's always kidding him about his advancing middle age." Then Tucker zeroed in on one of the secrets of the Regis and Kathie Lee draw: "If all this were merely playful, it would be insufferable, but there's a tinge of nastiness in this duo's sniping that keeps you wondering who's hurting whose feelings more." He concluded his review by commenting that the guests on *Live! With Regis & Kathie Lee* are almost incidental because "one tunes in . . . to listen to the edgy, amusing bickering."

Jeff Jarvis, *People*'s television critic, admitted that, "like oysters, blue cheese and rubber-soled shoes, Regis Philbin grew on me. . . . I'll be honest. I started watching the show not by choice but by force; my only real alternative was Geraldo. But to my surprise, I actually started to like Regis." Although Jarvis compared Philbin to "a game-show host with no prizes . . . like Donald O'Connor without the mule," he went on to say that Regis is "also witty, if harmlessly so. He can insult guests and get away with it." But Jarvis was far less benign about Kathie Lee, whom he thought "tries to be *sooo* perfect, a credit to her alma mater (Oral Roberts U.). If she had a twin, she'd be on one of those Doublemint gum commercials. She talks about her interior decoration, her country home and her parties as if we all had lives like hers. She cannot face anything approximating reality without putting on her *oh-yucky!* face and making a bit of a fool of herself." However, Jarvis took some of the sting out of his comments by admitting later in his review that Kathie Lee was growing on him. "Maybe Regis is making me like her. Yes, he can make you like his show in spite of yourself. Just as Bob Costas is well suited to his hour, Regis is perfectly suited to his. He's easy to take in the morning and that's not easy to be."

Jarvis's capitulation on Kathie Lee was reflected in the feelings of viewers. Alice Gatti wrote, "I could not have agreed more with Jeff Jarvis' review of *Live! With Regis & Kathie Lee* if I had written it myself. Regis does grow on you, but Kathie Lee, never. Perhaps my favorite moment was when she was having her broken fingernail repaired as her husband, Frank Gifford, looked adoringly on. I could barely swallow my raisin bran." And Stuart Greenblatt penned in Gifford's defense, "I totally disagree with Jeff Jarvis' opinion of Kathie Lee Gifford. I find her enlightening and enjoyable to watch. She adds humor to even the most boring segments. She may be sweet, but she doesn't leave a cavity in this mouth. I'm sure the rest of the country will agree."

They did. Within two years of the syndication debut, *Live! With Regis & Kathie Lee* was the fastest-growing national talk show in the country. Critics were confounded. What was so engaging about these two bickering hosts? Part of it was the sheer lack of embarrassment either showed. Kathie Lee had no qualms telling tittering tales about her love life with Frank. And Regis reveled in describing in graphic detail the minute-by-minute chronology of passing a kidney stone and loved to talk about his wife's family. "I realize there is nothing I can do about it," Joy admitted. "But there have been times that I have literally screamed at the TV."

Regis was unfazed. "Here's the trap you give yourself when you make your life part of the show," he explained in 1992 to Jess Cagle of *Entertainment Weekly*. "When something extraordinary happens to you and everybody knows about it, you gotta come back and tell them about it. When the doctor pulled out the tube, I said, 'I gotta have this because they won't believe it!' The audience doesn't want to know how wonderful your life is. What's going to keep them tuned in is the other side of life – the aggravations, the slights, the family stuff.

Sometimes you really gotta suck it up and tell the most embarrassing things."

Interestingly, even in the beginning, Kathie Lee seemed to gain more opportunities from the show's success than did Regis. Gifford was suddenly Ms. Spokeswoman, appearing on commercials and in print ads. Of course, her main gig was still Carnival Cruises, in which she chirped "If they could see me now" while twirling around the ship. Whether her appeal had any influence or not, in 1989 Carnival Cruise Lines became the largest and fastest-growing cruise line in the world. Coincidence? Gifford supporters would say no.

Any doubts about her growing kingdom should have been dispelled when *TV Guide* ran a Most Beautiful Woman on TV phone-in poll. Gifford was unabashedly determined to win, and for five days she begged viewers to vote for her. When the results were tallied, it was no contest. Gifford won hands down, and her closest competitor, Jaclyn Smith, trailed by over 14,000 votes. Some critics and industry insiders complained about her blatant abuse of power, but in her mind she'd won fair and square. "I didn't do anything illegal," she said at a press conference, dismissing the criticism.

While Regis used the show as a stage on which to perform and entertain, Gifford developed a more personal agenda within her stated desire to entertain. In her autobiography, she says, "I'm convinced our show has tapped into a need these days for normalcy, honesty, and good, clean, self-effacing nonsense. Much of our mail comes from patients in hospitals who watch us right before chemotherapy and from people in a lot of pain and suffering. 'Thank you,' they say, 'for helping me through the hardest time in my life.' Knowing we're doing some good is so rewarding to both Regis and me. We're not curing cancer or AIDS, but I'm all for the healing people derive through laughter."

Sometimes, along with the laughter, there were moments

of live television that left both Regis and Kathie Lee speechless, such as when Zsa Zsa Gabor went on the air and called entertainment reporter Claudia Cohen (then the wife of megabucks Revlon chief Ron Perelman) a bitch in front of millions of viewers. "I had no idea the cameras were on," Gabor claimed later at a press conference.

But out-of-control guests made live television a kick for Regis. In the coming years, though, he'd find out that being a national success brought scrutiny and exposure that were decidedly less enjoyable. And not only would he have to deal with his own troubles with the press, but he'd also get caught in the crossfire of Kathie Lee's ongoing battle with the media.

JAMES McGOON / LIAISON AGENCY

5

Triumphs and Troubles

There were times, especially in the early years of *Live! With Regis & Kathie Lee*, when Regis was in danger of being eclipsed by Kathie Lee because of what frequently seemed to be self-promotion. While the whole point of host chat was to establish a running, almost stream-of-consciousness, dialogue that focused on either what had happened in the hours since they last chatted or something in the news, the way that Gifford spouted off about her home life rubbed many people the wrong way. When Regis talked about his life, it seemed to be more well rounded. While his comments contained references to his family, it didn't seem like he was trying to present himself in any particular light, yet Kathie Lee could come across exactly the way she said she didn't want to: "Don't you wish you had my life? My perfect husband? My romantic, fairy-tale marriage? My lifestyle?" Philbin knew the chemistry he and Kathie had been so successful at presenting could easily go south if he let the balance between them shift too much. So it seemed to fall to Regis to rein in Kathie Lee when she began to climb too much on her personal soapbox.

But sometimes all Regis could do was stand aside, such as when Kathie Lee announced she was pregnant, because he knew the announcement would be a ratings gold mine for the show. Indeed, ratings around the country increased as moms and would-be moms followed each step of the pregnancy. No aspect of her pregnancy went unscrutinized, whether it be tender nipples, body changes, and even the baby's conception, which Gifford said happened on a cruise off the coast of Italy. The audience was so enthralled partly because Gifford had always said Frank, who had three grown children from his first marriage, to Maxine Ewart, and five grandchildren already, didn't really want to start a new family. And she had expressed worry that a child would ruin their "romance." But while sailing the Mediterranean, Kathie Lee had miscalculated her "rhythm" and later found herself pregnant.

Regis used significant airtime to try to convince the Giffords to name their baby after him, and his request generated plenty of banter between him and Kathie Lee. According to a newswire report, he said, "I threw out Xavier once too, which is my confirmation name, but they didn't go for it, so I guess I struck out twice. Hey, I'm just a co-host." A cohost who could smell ratings. He threw Gifford a baby shower on the show and greeted her nearing due date with typical Philbin fervor.

However, expectant mother or not, Gifford still managed to annoy people. In January 1990, Peter Castro reported in *People* that Kathie Lee had learned she was going to have a son. "After we found out it was a boy," Gifford was quoted as saying, "I was a little disappointed, but I remember Frank saying to me one night, 'Honey, maybe it's better that it's a boy, because he'll be here to take care of you when I'm gone.' And that really devastated me, because I don't like to think of my husband as ever being gone. He's unbelievably fit and robust, so I never think of him as growing older to the point that he'll someday probably pass away before I do. But that's the way he thinks. 'She'll have a son who'll take care of her.' It really represents the kind of human being I'm married to." It also represented a stereotype that had some people grinding their teeth. One reader of *People*, Diana Martone, noted, "When Kathie Lee Gifford's husband, Frank, announced it was better that their expected baby is a boy because 'he'll be here to take care of you when I'm gone,' she said, 'It really shows what kind of human being I'm married to.' It sure does. One who thinks that a woman can't survive unless there's a man around *taking care of her.* Wake up, Kathie Lee, and tell Frank who really does the *caretaking* in this world."

Eight hours after the baby was born by cesarean section on March 22, 1990, following a 16-hour labor, Kathie Lee was on the phone to Regis during the broadcast and told viewers they'd named him Cody Newton. She and Frank had chosen the name Cody after seeing Cleveland Browns tackle Cody Risien play in a game the previous fall. During her first week back on the show, Regis introduced the littlest Gifford: "This baby belongs to the *Regis and Kathie Lee* family. We'll be able to watch little Cody grow up together." Although Regis might later regret that sentiment, Cody's introduction earned a local 41 share, meaning that almost half of all viewers in New York City were watching.

Now when Kathie Lee talked, it wasn't just about Frank; now she had the whole of motherhood to bring to the table. And she didn't hesitate to speak out as a new mom. "Who can pretend this stuff doesn't affect the way our children will shape tomorrow's world?" she asked in her autobiography. "They can't read, they're gorged with junk food, they stare at MTV and play with their joysticks, Game Boys, and computers. It's terrifying. I don't want to use my show as a pulpit, but as a citizen and a mother, I feel compelled to say that I regard a lot of what's going on as flat-out disgusting."

By 1991, *Live! With Regis & Kathie Lee* was the fastest-growing talk show in the country, and affiliates were using it to shore up their morning schedules. One of the affiliates moving

Live! to a more prominent time slot was KABC in Los Angeles. In a bittersweet irony for Philbin, the show being cancelled to make room for *Live!* was *A.M. Los Angeles*, which had been airing on KCAL in Los Angeles up to then. And, in an even greater irony, the host of *A.M. Los Angeles* was none other than Steve Edwards, who'd got the *A.M. Chicago* job Philbin had so desperately wanted several years before. What made the decision to replace *A.M. Los Angeles* with *Live!* so surprising was that the former show was regularly beating the latter show in the ratings. But KABC executives decided that *A.M. Los Angeles* was simply too expensive to remain in production, costing the affiliate between $7 and $8 million a year. Adding *Live! With Regis & Kathie Lee* would save KABC more than 50%. "Cap Cities needs to cut back and we're where they do it," Edwards said at the time in an article by Dennis McDougal in the *Los Angeles Times*. "By canceling us, they get rid of a lot of bodies and roll the tape." Edwards's cohost, Tawny Little, also noted that returning to KABC was something "Regis has wanted to do forever." Philbin didn't dispute the statement, but he tried to downplay its significance and the vindication it brought. "I don't know if I call returning to KABC a personal triumph," Regis commented, adding, "I had done the show in Los Angeles and I always did want to try it nationally. They were pretty angry with me when I left," for his failed NBC morning show. If Edwards felt any resentment, he swallowed it. Instead, he expressed concern for the future of local programming, which both he and Regis had to thank for their respective careers. "When I started out," Edwards mused to McDougal, "we did all kinds of things. . . . I got to take camera crews all over the world. You don't have any of that today. Not in local programming."

Live! With Regis & Kathie Lee was succeeding at a time when talk shows in general were beginning to shift in tone and focus. In the coming years, hosts such as Jerry Springer, Sally Jesse Raphael, Ricki Lake, and Geraldo Rivera would usher in an era of titillation television, in which everyday people would try to outdo one another with sordid and sensational tales of their lives with topics such as videotaped indiscretions, ménages à trois, promiscuous teens, and mate swappers. "That was the year of discontent on television," Philbin would say to Jess Cagle of *Entertainment Weekly* in July 1992 about the later 1980s. "Geraldo was breaking his nose, Phil was walking around in a dress, Sally was walking around with hookers, Oprah was losing 65 pounds. And here we were talking about what we did last night! Who cared? But I knew that if they could just watch us two, three times in a row, that we could hook our share of the audience. And we did."

Although the sensational nature of these other talk shows attracted audiences, Regis and Kathie Lee's fan base was stronger, larger, and more loyal. "Three cheers for Kathie Lee and Regis," wrote Connie Smith in *People*. "Their impromptu banter is priceless, and their spontaneity and originality without comparison. They are like a breath of fresh air after listening to other talk shows laden with perverts and misfits pleading for understanding and would-be authors telling nasty secrets about their friends and families."

On *Live! With Regis & Kathie Lee*, the biggest controversy was whether or not Gifford was using her child as a self-promotional tool. "While Mr. Philbin can be camp and sardonically witty, Kathie Lee Gifford is nothing more than a huckster, hyping herself, her husband and her child ad nauseam," complained Christine Derdarin to *People*. "She smugly doles out snippets of her oh-so-privileged life to be experienced vicariously by a less-blessed audience. Hard to imagine being so well-paid for screeching *Reege*! at 30-second intervals." Elizabeth Sporkin and Sue Carswell of *People* similarly noted, "Even when they're not saying anything funny, they make you think there is substance under the bubbles. Consider this recent exchange after Philbin tripped on a cobblestone:

PHILBIN: I could feel myself spinning out of control!
GIFFORD: Reege!
PHILBIN: Usually I'm agile and I can handle it.
GIFFORD: Reege!
PHILBIN: There are hundreds of people looking. One guy said, "Oh, that's that Regis Philbin"!

Their point was that, regardless of little substance, they had something far more important – chemistry: "A mixture that attracts some 18 million fans weekly, including Mike Wallace and Madonna, who asked to be a guest in May. Says late-night host Arsenio Hall: 'You ain't hip unless you watch Regis and Kathie Lee.'"

And, while Regis basked in the glow of viewer adulation, Kathie Lee used her newfound status to resurrect her dormant music career. In the spring of 1991, she appeared at a two-week singing engagement at New York's tony Rainbow and Stars cabaret. Thanks to her constant on-air promotion, every performance was sold out, and Gifford reveled in the attention. According to Cagle in April 1991, Kathie Lee was almost giddy during her performances, telling the audience, "I can't rap, I just can't," and would explain she intended to perform "my favorite happy songs."

While she worked her pipes, Regis indulged in his own pet projects, such as popping up as a cohost, with Marla Maples, on *Wrestlemania VII*. In his autobiography, he mentions his helpless fascination with professional wrestling. "Joy doesn't understand it. Neither does Kathie Lee. But I can't help it. I have acute wrestlemania. I love wrestlers, love the noise they make, venting and spewing and challenging their opponents." Qualities, he then jokes, he also had to master in order to cohost with Gifford.

The show continued to cement their status as a pop cultural phenomenon by attracting guests such as Madonna, who showed up in May 1991 in a black negligee, explaining to Regis,

"I always look good in my nightgown." While Madonna can intimidate interviewers (think of David Letterman), Philbin happily held his own – and acted as a straight man when asking her, "What do you talk about with Michael Jackson?" Madonna jokingly replied, "Well, first I beg him not to wear his sunglasses, and, of course, he complies, because I am much stronger than he is. And then we exchange powder puffs. We both powder our noses and compare bank accounts."

Live! With Regis & Kathie Lee also became the favorite venue for celebrities to make surprise announcements. During an appearance on the show, longtime *Tonight Show* announcer Ed McMahon revealed he and advertising executive Pamela Hurn had been married in a spur-of-the-moment ceremony and introduced his new bride to the stunned cohosts.

Even negative publicity worked in their favor, such as when New York Transportation Commissioner Lou Riccio criticized Regis and Kathie Lee for complaining on national TV about the streets in Manhattan's Central Park West. Riccio claimed that, when he tried to call Philbin's office, he was put on hold. He was then told that Philbin was in a meeting, but Regis passed along the message that anything said was said for entertainment value. That appeased the commissioner – until the next time. "They did it again!" Anthony Scaduto and coauthors reported in *Inside New York* in November 1992. "We understand they even said we wouldn't have the nerve to call him. We did call him and he never called back! Although we understand the inconvenience, we have been telling people to avoid the area. I think it's outrageous that we're trying to get our message out there and working as quickly as we can to repair as much as we can, and he's trashing us."

The anecdote reveals a lesser-known side of Regis: the hard-nosed element of his personality. It was also on display when Philbin was invited to attend a lavish party on the yacht *The Spirit of New York* to celebrate Geraldo Rivera's 1,000th episode. Fellow talk show hosts Phil Donahue, Montel Williams, Sally Jesse Raphael, Maury Povich, and Joan Rivers were in attendance, but neither Regis nor Oprah Winfrey attended. As one Geraldo staffer mentioned to *Inside New York* in September 1992, "They're all personal friends, but business is business – and this is war."

Perhaps the most notable indication of the Regis and Kathie Lee juggernaut was their cohosting of the venerable Miss America Contest, with an estimated viewing audience in excess of 45 million people. Pageant officials hoped Gifford and Philbin would add a fresh approach to the ceremony, which had been hosted by Gary Collins since 1982. Before Collins, former television Tarzan Ron Ely hosted the pageant for two years, having replaced longtime host Bert Parks after he was controversially dumped in 1980.

Although Regis was thrilled at the significance of the gig, he tried to be humble. "Our humor can be acerbic. Why do I want to inflict myself on this institution? I look cross-eyed at Miss Arkansas and the whole thing goes boom," Regis joked to Ileane Rudolph of *TV Guide*. Actually, Philbin admitted he wouldn't mind spicing up the normally staid telecast with a little something unexpected. "We've been through every mishap you can imagine on television," he told Rudolph. "We wouldn't mind if that happened. That would be great."

However, when meeting with the press, Philbin kept his fantasies of on-air disasters to himself. "It's a thrill!" he said. "When you're a kid, you never dream that one day you'll be hosting the Miss America Pageant." Kathie Lee added that "working with Regis is like being on a trapeze. I can't wait to see his reaction to working with 50 bright, beautiful and accomplished young women in Atlantic City."

A month after the nation was treated to hearing Regis and Kathie Lee sing a duet of "There She Goes," papers around the country carried a small item that Gifford was lending her name to a modestly priced clothing line. According to fashion industry trade papers, the line was expected to bring in more than $10 million in sales its first year. The same columns reported that cartoonist Gary Trudeau was joining with a mail-order company to develop *The Great Doonesbury Sellout* catalog that would sell merchandise ranging from leather bomber jackets to T-shirts. Trudeau would donate all his royalties and a portion of the company's revenues to a group of charities. However, Gifford was making no such commitment, the clothing line apparently intended to be a money-making venture for her – an issue that would later come back to dog her.

But as 1992 dawned, all was right in the *Live! With Regis & Kathie Lee* world. Regis had settled into a comfortable schedule that seldom varied during the workweek. He would get up at 7:30 and "take a tablespoon of cod-liver oil and two tablespoons of milk for my arthritis. I take my shower, shave, have some breakfast, go back and brush my teeth." At the time, he and Joy were living in a three-bedroom Park Avenue apartment with their two daughters, both on the cusp of adulthood. At work, he and Kathie Lee had developed a sometimes uneasy but workable coexistence. "We've never had a fight, not even a cross word," Regis frequently said. Likewise, Gifford's mantra explaining the secret of their success was, "We don't take ourselves too seriously. And we have a lot of fun at each other's expense."

While Philbin and Gifford may have enjoyed being the butt of each other's jibes, it was much less fun being on the receiving end of negative or embarrassing publicity in the tabloid press. The first assault began shortly after the show went into syndication when the *National Enquirer* ran an article in 1989 that claimed Philbin's son, Danny, had been abandoned by his father and was living with Kay in an LA housing project. Regis called the report nothing but lies and said Danny was living comfortably in the San Fernando Valley and working as a political intern.

Regis dreaded Danny being brought up in any context because of the struggle every day of his life had been. "He's my hero in life," an emotional Philbin told *Esquire*'s Bill Zehme in 1994. "For him to overcome all this disability, to graduate from college, work on his master's program – he's just dynamite, a remarkable kid. Now he's got a permanent job coming up. But it's been a grind. I remember for one year straight he was in the hospital, and I'd go see him every day. I'll tell you, anytime he goes back into the hospital it's like a knife in my heart. I wish it were me, not him."

Regis spoke at greater length during an on-line interview with Paul Harris on July 22, 1997, helping to promote The Paul Harris Comedy Concert for Children's Hospital, explaining that he prefers to keep certain aspects of his life private. "That's how I have felt about it all these years and I think, I know, Dan does, too, and that is how we chose to keep it, you know?" He added, in what seemed to be a mild shot directly at Kathie Lee, who'd have made Danny's setbacks and successes the grist for constant chatter on the show, "There are a lot of celebrities who would use something like this, frankly, for their own publicity purposes. That is not my cup of tea."

During the interview, though, Regis did recall Danny's experience at Children's Hospital in Los Angeles. "I guess both of us will never forget that. It was one thing after another that prevented him from leaving and it was frustrating and depressing and I was going down there five days a week. It just broke my heart not to be able to take him out. And this would go on day after day, and week after week, and month after month. So I know what it is like to be at a children's hospital and to see those kids in pain."

To Philbin, it was simple: he believed that, if he were to talk extensively about Danny's problems, people would feel pity for his malady rather than pride over his accomplishments. And

Regis couldn't abide pity. "Dan doesn't want it, and I don't, either," he emphasized.

Making the *National Enquirer* article more painful was when Howard Stern picked up on it and mounted a Danny Philbin Radiothon. "That was the worst time," Gifford indignantly told Zehme in 1994. "It was the cruelest, nastiest, most dishonest story. And then to make fun of it! You could burn in hell for that." Regis took a more tempered stance. "Howard Stern is probably a nice guy. But I'm not going to go on the radio with him and defend myself. I mean, who would it help?" Interestingly, Danny responded to the accusations against his father by simply telling *People*, "I love my dad, and I'm really proud of him."

There were other reports Regis chose not to respond to, such as when the *Globe* reported in February 1996 that Kay Faylen had complained to friends, "All I ever got out of Regis was a little money and two kids. While he lives like a king, I've spent the years struggling to raise my kids on the $300 a month he gave me."

Although most people would dismiss the stories, even if true, as the typical aftermath of a divorce, another story reported in the *Globe* wasn't so easily ignored. While Danny struggled to overcome his physical disability, Philbin's daughter Amy fought to surmount a more insidious hurdle – drugs. By the early 1990s, Amy Philbin was struggling to get by, living with her musician husband, Dan Ferguson, and their young son, Mack, in a rundown duplex in Studio City, California. An associate of Amy described her perilous existence for the *Globe* in 1993: "She's a binge drinker. She will go days or even weeks without getting drunk, then lose all control and go on a three-day bender. She'll go through bottle after bottle of cheap vodka and use what little cash she has left over to buy cocaine." When she was on a bender, Amy would drop Mack off with her husband's parents so the little boy wouldn't be present when she flew into rages, ripping telephone cords from walls or arguing with her husband. A friend said much of Amy's fury stemmed from unresolved emotions over her parents' divorce and feelings of abandonment – emotions Amy seemed unable to confront her father with directly. Most of her contact with Regis seemed to come when she needed help.

"Amy and her husband get by, but barely," a friend noted in the *Globe* article. "Dan's a good musician and does studio work whenever he can get it. But he's out of work more often than not. More than once, Amy has been so desperate that she's swallowed her pride and called Regis for money. And he does send it, although not a lot. And Regis has come out to see Mack a couple of times, but the visits are always tense and usually send Amy into another drinking binge." Amy would also be arrested for a DUI and have her license suspended later for failure to comply with the terms of her sentence.

In the years following publication of the article that outlined Amy's troubles, Regis would reach out to his daughter and son-in-law by hiring them to write music for both an audio walking tape he recorded and an exercise video and encourage Amy to pursue her dream of making it as a singer, which Philbin says has always been her passion. In his autobiography, Regis only hints at any remorse he might feel. "I used to occasionally take Amy to the [Joey Bishop] show with me when it was taped earlier in the evening. She looked like a pretty little waif back then. . . . After Joy and I were married, she came to live with us for awhile and later decided to go her own way. I always wished I could have done more for her. I still do."

Gifford also had personal tragedies, which she shared with the *Live! With Regis & Kathie Lee* audience. On August 31, 1992, Kathie Lee announced that she'd recently suffered a miscarriage. "Frank and I were planning our second baby to be . . . to come . . . this fall . . . this spring. . . . I just wanted to tell everybody myself. Until you experience it (a miscarriage) yourself, you really don't understand the heartbreak of it." She assured the stunned audience that "It hasn't discouraged me. We're going to try for a while longer – if Frank would just stay in town. I don't think it's my last chance."

Gifford's ability to make such an announcement and within minutes turn the tables and offer her fans comfort and reassurance was a significant factor in her popularity. At these moments, Philbin would wisely fade into the background, knowing anything he'd say would be superfluous. It was better to be quiet and supportive and let Gifford have the moment. Understanding the best way to complement her in any particular situation was one of his unheralded strokes of genius. But just as he can offer calm reassurance and encouragement in emotional moments, he offers comic relief and vaudeville during personal appearances. And as the duo's popularity grew, so did their personal appearances.

So great was the demand that Gifford and Philbin developed a show and took it to the road, playing venues such as the Westbury Music Fair and in Las Vegas. The *Live! with Regis & Kathie Lee* tour consisted of Regis doing a sort of stand-up routine using recent newspaper clippings, Gifford and Philbin talking to each other, and Kathie Lee singing. Regis was annoyed at times when people expressed surprise that he'd been performing in a stage show. "People for years thought: 'What do you do? Do you cook an egg?'" But then he shrugged away the thought by reverting to form in a press conference. "What does *Sinatra* do? What does *Tony Bennett* do?"

Once again, the duo was asked to host the Miss America Pageant. This time around, there was a little controversy to pep up the proceedings. For the first time in the Miss America Pageant, AIDS awareness was given a showcase in the hope of sending a message to the mainstream audience. Regis and some

of the guest judges wore the red ribbons signifying AIDS awareness on their lapels. And the eventual winner got a rousing
reception when she said she'd like to take her AIDS awareness
platform into schools and churches. And that winner? None
other than Leanza Cornett, at the time a 21-year-old Rollins
College communications major who'd go on to make a name for
herself in television broadcasting as a cohost of *Entertainment
Tonight.* But as Elizabeth Wasserman reported in *Newsday,* "the
ribbon on co-host Kathie Lee Gifford's hip, and on the breasts
of so many Miss America wannabees, does suggest that perhaps
Americans are finally coming to realize that AIDS is a disease, at
once like, and unlike, any other."

While Regis used his spare time to participate in fun events
such as cohosting with Joan Lunden the *Walt Disney World
Very Merry Christmas Parade,* which aired Christmas morning
in 1992 on ABC, Gifford spent her time writing a memoir with
Jim Jerome titled *I Can't Believe I Said That!* In it, she gave the
Kathie Lee version of her life, including her marriage to Paul
Johnson. She promoted the book as only Kathie Lee could,
mentioning it on *Live! With Regis & Kathie Lee* any chance she
got, which elicited sighs and rolling eyes from Regis. But he
knew not to say anything negative, and shortly after its release
it went to fourth spot on the best-seller list, behind Rush
Limbaugh, Madonna, and General Schwarzkopf, causing Gifford
to note she was "in good company, with corn, porn, and Stormin'
Norm!" It went back to print five times in three weeks for a
total of 255,000 copies.

In interviews to promote the book, Gifford presented herself as a perennial victim who'd endured untold suffering. "I
would sob for hours about certain incidents," Elizabeth Gleick
and Sue Carswell quoted her in *People,* noting that her eyes
brimmed with tears as she talked. "I've suffered in ways that
are perhaps going to be surprising to people. But my message

is: Trust God with your life, and He'll make something beautiful out of it. It may take a long time, but He will."

Her popularity almost threatened to eclipse that of Regis as Kathie Lee seemed to be incapable of doing any wrong in the eyes of her fans. So fertile was her appeal that *McCall's* took what was then seen as a gamble by replacing the magazine's traditional gingerbread-house cover with a smiling shot of Gifford, only to see its newsstand sales skyrocket to the highest of the year. Not to be outdone, *Redbook* would put Gifford on its cover six months later and sold 130,000 more copies than it had the previous July. Soon it was de rigueur to have Kathie Lee on the cover, with *Ladies' Home Journal* and *Good Housekeeping* following suit.

But Regis had reason to crow too, for 1992 was a significant milestone for him. He was celebrating his 30th year in show business, and the occasion made him reflect on his successes and his failures during that time. He told Cagle that, while he was "always the punching bag of the press, just to be on top now makes you forget all that." His biggest disappointment was his "inability to cash in on the opportunities that came my way. I should've grabbed that Westinghouse show and run with it and been on top for the next thirty years. Johnny Carson was in the same place at the same time and became a national icon. And me? I've been hustling, trying to make ends meet."

While Regis didn't have to worry about keeping a roof over his head anymore, he didn't stop hustling and acting as if the wolf was stalking outside his door. And that work ethic would eventually open the door for a level of success he surely thought wasn't possible.

6

Various Predicaments

Getting older is a deceptive process. Although we're vaguely aware that our bodies aren't as spry as they used to be, inside our heads we don't feel all that much different. Although in 1993 Regis was in his fifties, he considered himself to be in good physical shape, being an avid tennis player and keeping his waistline trim. But, like a lot of people in his generation, his eating habits weren't the best. He still preferred a hamburger from the network cafeteria for lunch as opposed to five servings of fruits and vegetables a day. But his attitude was about to undergo a serious adjustment.

Regis was shooting a commercial aboard a Carnival Cruise Lines ship in Florida when he began having chest pains. Not wanting to draw undue attention to himself and no doubt a little embarrassed, Philbin fought through the pain and finished the commercial without telling anyone of his discomfort. But that evening he couldn't bear the pain and eventually landed in a hospital, where doctors informed him that one of his arteries was almost completely blocked by plaque. He needed an angioplasty immediately.

"I had a blocked artery. The great thing about it was that all the people sitting at home, watching on the couch, feeling the same thing . . . got up and called the doctor. I still get letters thanking me for saving people's lives," Regis said. He would also later tell the *Record*'s Evonne Coutros that "I have a new appreciation of diet and exercise," which prompted him to put out an exercise tape. "First of all, exercise tapes are usually made for women. This is made for men *and* women."

In an irony not lost on Regis, the day he was scheduled to return to *Live! With Regis & Kathie Lee* from his week's sick leave after the angioplasty he was booked to appear on *Good Morning America* to plug a cookbook "coauthored" by him and Gifford – *Cooking with Regis and Kathie Lee* – filled with cholesterol-packed recipes. When asked if the book was approved by the American Heart Association, Philbin retorted, "I don't even know if it's approved by Kathie Lee." He also joked, "What's this about the book – an investigative report? Now I'm responsible for everybody?"

Actually, the appearance to promote the book was taped before Philbin underwent the angioplasty. So, feeling newly responsible, he appeared in person after the taped segment was broadcast to talk about his medical close call and how it had prompted him to change some elements of his life. All humility aside, Regis knew that, by going on the air and talking about his problem, he could inspire others to have check-ups or start watching how they ate. In other words, he truly had the ability to save lives. Such a realization was enough to make even Regis pause. For a while, anyway.

Not just wanting to put out a book with his name on it, Philbin told the *Good Morning America* viewers that the recipes had all been prepared on *Live! With Regis & Kathie Lee* and that he and Gifford had personally sampled the results. *Live!*'s executive producer, Michael Gelman, told Ben Kubasik of *Newsday*, "When I picked the recipes for the show in the book, I tried to have things cooked for health. But everybody doesn't want just healthy recipes. So there's a chapter on delicious des-

Regis at bat

Regis and his wife, Joy, at a celebrity tennis match, 1996

Regis, Joy, and their daughter, 1998

Regis and Kathie Lee in Florida, 1997

Regis shooting a workout video in New York City, 1998.

Regis and Randy "Macho Man" Savage

serts that have a high fat content." Keeping his current situation in mind, Philbin said perhaps he'd lay off the taste testing for a while. "Let Kathie Lee try them," he joked. "She's only pregnant."

Yes, Gifford had recently announced to him and the world that she and Frank were expecting another baby later that summer, so once again fans were abuzz with the new addition to the *Live!* family. But if there was any question about the importance of Regis to the show, it was answered by one quick look at the ratings on February 1, the day of his return from surgery. The local ratings earned a 35 share, and beyond that his comeback gave Regis his highest 28-market Nielsen ratings that year. He was loved. And he was trusted. According to a survey done at the time, Philbin ranked in the top 10 of America's most believable celebrity pitch people. In other words, he was about to become much sought after by advertisers of health-care products. Suddenly, Kathie Lee was getting a run for her money in the spokesperson department.

Some, though, thought Regis should slow down, at least when it came to his extracurricular activities. But Philbin denied he was a workaholic. "It's not an addiction," he said of his frequently hectic schedule. "It's just that things catch up with you. I say yes to something six months in advance and before I know it, every weekend it seems to be something." But he also told Bill Zehme of *Esquire* in 1994, "You know what they say: If you stop, you're dead." On the same subject, he mentioned to Curt Schleier of the *Minneapolis Star Tribune* that perhaps "it's my Notre Dame years, striving for perfection. Maybe it was my Catholic-school upbringing and guilt – 'Don't slack off, do the best you can.' I don't know how to answer that."

The call to slow down was reinforced that May when Regis was hospitalized for tests after he experienced heaviness in his chest. No doubt playing in his mind were the doctors' warnings that angioplasties don't always hold up and need to be repeated. While waiting for the test results, Philbin videotaped a message for the *Live! With Regis & Kathie Lee* audience of May 13, 1993. "It's just a little heaviness, not anything like last time, but enough to make me call my doctor. He urged me to come in so we can take a little picture to check it out. . . . I hate going through this. But I'm fine, really. I mean who's in better shape than me? What Frank Gifford would give to look like this! So, please, no calls, no flowers, no cards. I'm fine. I'll be back on the show Monday." Gelman told Kubasik that Regis "was mad at himself because he thinks he made too much of the heaviness."

If Regis thought he had problems, though, they were nothing compared with the woes of an actress he knew named Andrea Evans. And, in a strange twist of fate, he figured peripherally in her bizarre tale. In the late 1980s, Evans was one of the top stars in daytime, playing Tina Clayton on *One Life to Live*, which shoots in New York. In 1987, she took her visiting parents to see what was then *The Morning Show*, on which she'd been a frequent guest. After the show, Regis commented to Evans that he'd gotten the letter she'd sent to him about the dog. The actress was mystified – she hadn't sent him any letter. When he showed her the note, she realized it had been sent by someone trying to pose as her but didn't give it that much thought. But then, she told Maria Eftimiades of *People*, "shortly after that I started getting fake legal documents in the mail about suing Regis. Of course, I disregarded those too."

But that autumn Evans was accosted in the lobby of the ABC studios in New York by some man who yelled at her about a dog. Although she called the police, there was really nothing authorities could do at the time since current antistalking laws hadn't been enacted. A couple of weeks later, the same man showed up at the studio where the soap filmed and slit his wrists on the front steps. This time the police hauled him off to the Bellevue, New York's infamous psychiatric hospital, where he listed Evans as his next of kin. After that, he started sending her death threats, which got the attention of the FBI because the same man had also threatened former president Ronald Reagan.

Even though the man was periodically treated for paranoid schizophrenia and institutionalized, inevitably he'd be released, and the cycle of stalking and threats would continue. Finally, Evans quit the soap in 1990 and moved away from Manhattan. Two years later, she was back in New York to participate in a celebrity tennis tournament and was invited to appear on *Live! With Regis & Kathie Lee.* As she was walking into the studio, she spotted the stalker in the crowd outside, and he started chasing her. She ran inside screaming for help, but guards failed to apprehend the guy. Evans stayed out of sight until 1999, when she resurfaced on the LA-based *The Bold and the Beautiful.*

The Evans experience was a reminder to both Regis and Kathie Lee that all it takes is one deranged fan out of the millions of benign viewers. Nonetheless, Gifford and Philbin didn't draw back from their fans. Typically, after the show wrapped up its telecast, Regis and Kathie Lee were enthusiastically but politely mobbed by audience members hoping for autographs. Regis also posed for photographs and some audience chat. Even during commercial breaks on the show, Philbin would trot off into the audience to mingle and make small talk. "I do that every day because I want to keep them up and myself up," he told Coutros. "I started doing it years ago when I was the announcer on *The Joey Bishop Show.* I understand the value of that."

That appreciation of his audience is one of Philbin's secrets of success. Regis reaches out to them, and they flock to see him. In addition to his gigs with Kathie Lee, he also began to perform as a solo act, putting together anecdotes, observations, and a little singing and piano playing into a fan-pleasing stage presentation. When Regis is without Gifford, Michael Gelman comes along as a kind of sidekick. And, once Philbin is comfortable with someone, he likes to have the person around as much as possible. It was the same philosophy when it came to choosing replacement cohosts for Kathie Lee when she went on maternity leave the second time. Network honchos debated bringing in a couple of celebrity fill-in hosts, but Regis wouldn't hear of it. He wanted his wife, Joy. He thought she knew the show and its cadences, she knew him, and the audience liked seeing them together. Even though he liked to give Joy little on-air jabs, there was nobody he'd rather have had as a temporary cohost, and his opinions now carried greater weight.

And most fans and critics agreed that Regis was right. "For any number of reasons – vacation, weather, diaper rash – Kathie Lee Gifford sometimes can't be there for Regis Philbin on *Live! With Regis & Kathie Lee*," wrote Jess Cagle of *Entertainment Weekly* in July 1991. "On those occasions, it's a joy to see Joy Philbin, Regis' wife of 24 years, take her place, because she knows how to torture him better even than Kathie Lee and can puncture his ego just by crossing her arms."

Joy explained their on-air chemistry to Cagle in 1994 by saying, just as with Gifford, "We never talk about what we're going to talk about." Joy also admitted getting a kick when people stop Regis on the street and ask him when she's coming back on the show, "because I'm always the one who hears, *Where's Regis?*" Retorted Regis, "It's getting on my nerves."

With Regis, though, usually the more grief he gives someone the more affection he feels for that person. Take Gelman. Despite all the grief Philbin gives his producer on the air, they are as close as family off camera. "I've told them enough about Gelman to make him a mythical creature," Regis joked to Cagle in 1991. So much so that at one point Michael had to get an unlisted number to stem the flow of marriage proposals and blind date offers he was getting. For over 10 years, Gelman put up with every devious idea Philbin came up with to annoy him, such as a nationwide Gelman Look-Alike Contest. "It'd be a scream, but he wimped out," Philbin told Cagle, adding, "We're gonna do it, I think, this November anyway." Other stunts dreamed up for Gelman have included being shot out of a circus cannon on West 67th Street in New York and bungee jumping from a crane 15 stories high.

Yet Philbin told Karen Thomas of usa Today, "I don't go out of my way to include him" in the show. "Either she [Gifford] gets mad at him, or I need a question answered. But he seems to be more and more part of the show." And, when the camera pans over to Gelman during host chat, the audience often sees someone wishing the camera isn't on him. "It's downright embarrassing," he admitted to Thomas. "I'm not there to look smart and interesting. Usually, they're asking me a question that is unanswerable, or no matter what I say, it's not going to be the right answer." The biggest misconception, he says, is that "people think my job consists of standing off to the side, smiling and nodding my head. And then I go home." Gifford, not surprisingly, had little sympathy for Gelman. As she said to Thomas, "You have to have a thick skin to work here. Everybody on our show takes good-natured ridicule."

All of Philbin's teasing and mischief making tends to mask the genuine affection Regis has for Gelman, who started as an intern prior to Regis's arrival at *The Morning Show* in the 1980s. Gelman left to finish his education when Regis was hired, returned after his graduation, and was given a job as a production assistant. Gelman rose through the ranks until he was in a position to produce, a turn of events Regis would have approved of wholeheartedly. But personality conflicts with the *Morning Show* producer at the time caused Gelman to leave and take a job at the game show *Hollywood Squares*. When he returned to New York, Regis hired him to produce his Lifetime show, and, when the next *Morning Show* producer left, Regis brought Gelman back on board as the man in charge. He was only 26.

"I consider him to be one of my closest friends," says Philbin, who spends much more time off camera with his producer than he ever has with his cohost. Regis and Michael have lunch together several times a week and speak on the phone nearly every evening to discuss the next morning's show. While being Philbin's foil may be Michael's biggest claim to fame, within the television industry Gelman has earned respect – and a little envy – from his peers. Talking about his boss, Gelman says, "He created a role for me on the show." As far as his own contribution goes, Michael says candidly, "I can take credit for giving them a format and highlighting their talent and we create situations for them to be funny, but I've wanted to produce since I was 8 years old."

Gelman says he spent much of his childhood in Highland Park, Illinois, taking home movies of his family. While a broadcast management major at the University of Colorado, which he chose because it offered the extracurricular activity of skiing, he landed a summer job at WABC in New York City in 1982. "I was probably one of those obnoxiously overzealous interns," he admitted to *People*'s Michael Lipton and Nancy Matsumoto. But through hard work, he says, he made himself "indispensable."

Regis is proud of Gelman the way a father would be of a son. "He's one of the smartest young people I've ever known." Even though Gelman started out as a wunderkind, Philbin notes in a press transcript, "This show has aged him. He operates under a lot of pressure and can gracefully withstand all of the daily problems. Thousands of guests are offered to us each year – some of them friends of ours – and Gelman is the only one who can say no. I couldn't do it. But he does it without impunity if he thinks they're not right for the show."

Gelman has also had to endure bouts of animosity from Gifford for daring on occasion to suggest she talk less about her children. "His body language!" she complained to Lipton and Matsumoto. "Oh, please. The minute I mention Cody it's like. . . . What I give Michael credit for is how hard he works and how much he cares," said Gifford, adding, "Regis likes the whole buddy thing."

But what Philbin also likes is that Gelman knows how to run the show Regis's way, and, as Mary Kellogg, an executive for syndicator Buena Vista Productions, notes in press material, "His first priority is the show. He eats, breathes, and sleeps this show." Which means he's willing to take on Gifford and face her wrath, which can be considerable. In an interview with Phil Rosenthal of the Los Angeles *Daily News* Kathie Lee spoke somewhat patronizingly of her producer. "Gelman and I have so little in common that there's always a battle, it seems, in terms of values, in terms of taste. We just rarely agree on anything. He tries to tell me what our audience wants and I laugh. I go, 'How do you know? . . . Don't tell me what a mother in Iowa with four children, who stays at home, wants to hear about.'"

According to Philbin, the tension between them also has to do with Gelman saying no to Gifford. As he said to Rosenthal, "Because Gelman is the producer, he decides who is booked as a guest and who isn't. Sometimes, though, Kathie Lee has disagreed with Gelman's ideas and it eventually created an icy wall between them. The breaking point, I think, came when Gelman refused to book Art Buchwald, an old pal of the Giffords. She pushed and pushed and Gelman wouldn't cave [in] and it seethed in her heart and just kept festering." Gifford and Gelman made up and played lovey-dovey on camera, but they will never be as close as Michael and Regis – they'll probably never even be friends. Nor will Gelman ever completely approve of the amount of airtime she spends talking about her children.

In August 1993, Gifford gave birth to an eight-pound, 11-ounce daughter, Cassidy Erin, at Greenwich Hospital in

Connecticut. In keeping with the tradition of sharing private moments with the nation, Frank Gifford called Regis on the air to give him the details of the birth. What Frank didn't mention was the embarrassing situation Kathie Lee found herself in with the unlikely personage of Larry Flynt, the notorious publisher of *Hustler* magazine.

The situation began when Gifford agreed to appear on the cover of the fall issue of *Maternity Fashion and Beauty*. It wasn't until after she'd shot the photo session that it came to her attention that the magazine's publisher was none other than Flynt, who publishes over 25 magazines in addition to *Hustler*, among them the blatantly nonerotic *PC Laptop Computers* and *Camera and Darkroom Photography*. Even so, not surprisingly, Gifford was horrified at being associated in any way with a man she considered a pornographer. Her attorney, Ronald Konecky, was quoted by Mark Goodman and Lyndon Stambler as saying, "She agreed to appear in a photo session that deals with maternity clothes. When we found out about Mr. Flynt's ownership, we tried to have her not be associated with the magazine or with the cover. Obviously she is disappointed and distressed about this." Nobody at the magazine sympathized with Gifford. "Kathie Lee Gifford did the May cover for *Longevity*, which is owned by (*Penthouse* publisher) Bob Guccione," noted *Maternity Fashion and Beauty*'s editor-in-chief, Linda Arroz, who also pointed out to Goodman and Stambler that Kathie Lee "was in a provocative pose on the *Longevity* cover as opposed to the innocent one on our cover." When it was suggested that Flynt's name on the masthead would be the kiss of death for the magazine, Flynt said dryly to Goodman and Stambler, "People are so naïve. If they thought I was going to put something in the maternity book that's going to offend someone, that would be ludicrous. It costs millions to launch a magazine that size. The question of Larry Flynt publishing a magazine for women can be answered only by the women who read the magazine.

Anybody who hasn't read it and wants to criticize it, I don't want to waste my time talking to them."

And, as if that predicament wasn't keeping Kathie Lee's lawyers busy enough, the Giffords next took on the *National Enquirer* after the tabloid reported Kathie Lee had been artificially inseminated with Frank's sperm in a "controversial" procedure to assure them that the couple would have a daughter. After the tab refused to print a retraction, Kathie Lee sued it, asking for $45 million in damages. She wouldn't get it, but just telling the world she was suing was part of the whole point.

This run-in with the *National Enquirer* reaffirmed Gifford's growing anger with certain elements of the media, which Kathie Lee thought were in some ways out to get her – especially mainstream critics. She became further incensed a short time later after receiving a drubbing at the hands of New York reviewers who slammed her performances at the Lincoln Center. She described the gig as "a triumph . . . standing ovations, curtain calls, everything. And the critics smeared me in their papers." As she told Rosenthal of the *Daily News*, if critics hated her that much and wanted her to go away that badly, "all they have to do is give me an unbelievably glowing review and I will die from shock and they will never have to worry about me again."

Ironically, though, even critics who didn't love Kathie Lee and Regis felt oddly compelled by them. Gail Pennington of the *St. Louis Post-Dispatch* tried to understand what it was that drew people. "This homey show, with a living room for a set and guests who are mostly celebrities promoting something, is so different from the rest of the talkers that it almost doesn't fit the category. On Monday hosts Regis Philbin and Kathie Lee Gifford chatted about their weekends. . . . Later, Gifford made sweet-and-sour chicken . . . and the two visited with guests Garth Brooks and Lesley Ann Warren. The appeal of all this is hard to explain, but the show has a huge following; in fact, I myself watch at least the first half almost every morning while getting ready for work. My notes say: 'Go figure.'"

Even the master of knowing good nothing when he sees it, Jerry Seinfeld, has commented on the show. "I, for one, couldn't be more impressed," Bill Zehme quoted him as saying in 1994. "You can't do less than they do and make a living."

Part of the fascination has been to see the number of entertainment and political figures who've popped up on the show. For example, First Lady Hillary Rodham Clinton all but invited herself to be a guest on *Live! With Regis & Kathie Lee* when she was in New York promoting her health plan. She had a few hours to spare, so White House staff contacted the show and asked if the First Lady could join the hosts. "Like we were going to say no," Regis said to Michael Shain and Pat Wechsler. Hillary later revealed her appearance was due to the prompting of her mother, a die-hard Philbin fan. For those watching, though, it was a fascinating glimpse into the White House, such as when Hillary described having to buy a table and chairs for the East Wing kitchen just for her family because the only other dining rooms in the White House were formal.

Regis showed why the First Lady's mother, Dorothy Rodham, was such a fan. He asked Hillary what her mother thought of Bill Clinton the first time Hillary took him home to meet the family. Hillary smiled and said, "I thought: 'Where's Arkansas?'" It was the kind of unexpected entertainment that kept fans tuning in and Regis and Kathie Lee *the* talk show hosts to visit. Philbin wasn't mean spirited and was mostly interested in everyone having a good time. And, as he'd done several times before, he was catching the attention of producers everywhere, especially those working in the field of late-night television.

At the end of 1993, the late-night landscape was a bitterly fought war filled with contenders who wanted to take over from a retired Johnny Carson as the Prince of Late Night. It was an ugly war that would end friendships, create bitter rivalries, and leave many casualties in its wake. Chevy Chase learned the ultimate lesson in humility – one with which Regis could identify – when his late-night entry for FOX was mercilessly skewered by critics and cancelled after just six weeks. Never daunted by failure, Hollywood's brain trust looked around for other suitable hosts to enter the fray and latched on to Philbin. The idea was that Regis would appeal to an older demographic, the way Carson had, thereby pulling in old Carson viewers disenchanted with his successor, Jay Leno. Philbin's agent, Jim Griffin, confirmed there had been talks and called the idea interesting, but he stressed that nothing was happening at the time.

Nor would it. If anyone could appreciate the sentiment of "Been there, done that," it was Regis. He'd been through the late-night talk show wars not once but twice and had barely escaped with his career. He was aware how fortunate he was to have *Live! With Regis & Kathie Lee*, and he wasn't about to abandon ship, even if he could contractually. After having a hard time initially adjusting to the move east, he and Joy were happy with their life in New York. He had the show down to a science, and he loved what he was doing. To leave the show then would have been to invite professional disaster. His dream had always been to do a show his way for a national audience, and that's what he had. He knew that, however green the grass of late-night television looked, it was only an illusion.

Besides, Regis was too wrapped up in the college football season to think about career changes. And, adding to his joy as 1993 drew to a close was the fact that his youngest daughter, J.J., was attending his alma mater, Notre Dame. She told Sue Carswell of *People* that she had vivid memories of her father's Irish fanaticism. "He was always talking about Knute Rockne and the Gipper," she said. But, she added, there was no pressure placed on either daughter to follow in their father's collegiate footsteps. "When I decided to go to Notre Dame, it was my decision. He was more ecstatic for me than he was for himself."

Which is not to say Regis doesn't still bleed Irish green. In fact, he has told Joy that when he dies his ashes are to be scattered over Notre Dame. "I think it appeals to his economic side," Joy joked to Zehme of *Esquire* in 1994. J.J. is apparently a chip off the old Philbin rah-rah block, because she exudes the same passion for her surroundings as her father did and still does. Watching her in his old environment makes the normally upbeat Philbin pause sentimentally. As he said to Sue Carswell, "It does my heart good to see my daughter as happy here as I was."

And for Regis the good times were only going to get better.

Regis and his daughter, JJ, 1998

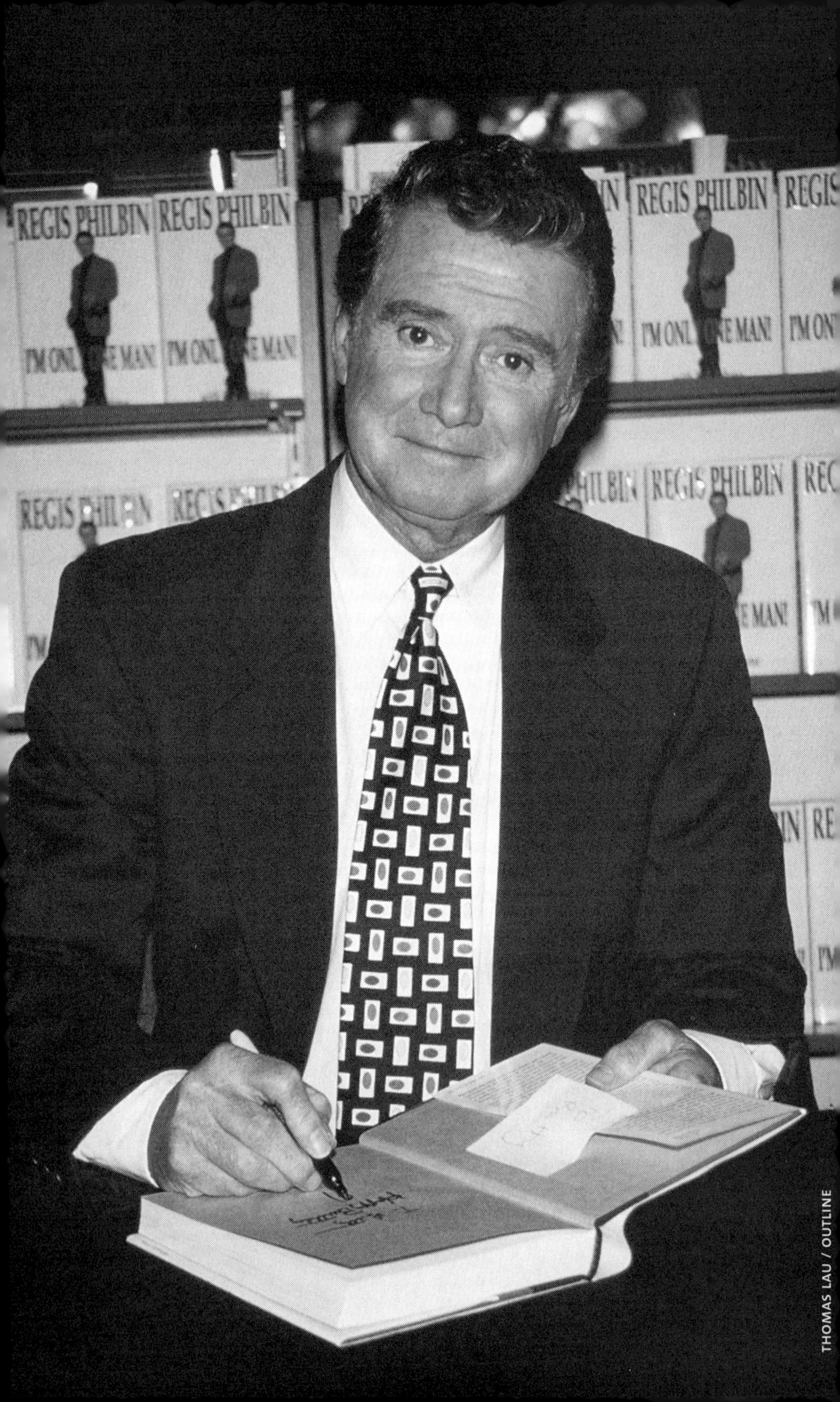

THOMAS LAU / OUTLINE

7

Rising
and
Falling

"I am the king!" When Regis Philbin says this, which is often enough, he does so with just enough tongue in cheek that nobody views him as an egomaniac on par with, say, James Cameron, who announced at the Oscars one year that he was king of the world. But when you're 60 years old and on the top of your career game, the number-one man in the daytime television universe, and admired by millions of fans, there is definite cause for celebration and a sense of well-being.

Dana Carvey, who proved just how central Regis is in pop culture by including an impression of him in his *Saturday Night Live* repertoire, gushed to Bill Zehme in 1994, "Regis embodies comedy in the classic form! He's the Put-Upon Guy, the guy who always gets the bad seat at the roast and isn't afraid to tell you about it. He has no pretense! He's totally honest on the air, and if you're totally honest, how are you not cool?" Ironically, Philbin's idol, Perry Como, also went through a career gentrification, with the younger generation deciding that longevity and talent are cool regardless of hair color.

Washington Post TV critic Tom Shales, according to press material from *Live! With Regis & Kathie Lee*, had these sage words of advice for Conan O'Brien when he took over *Late*

Night with Conan O'Brien: "Watch Regis . . . his ability to make entertainment out of nothing, to bound onto the air day after day, always personable and amusing."

But if there was an ultimate stamp of hipness, it came from David Letterman. "He's just about the best there is at what he does," Letterman told Zehme in 1994. "It must be odd to be his age and be at the top of your game. He just wears me out." Of Letterman, Philbin said to Paul Harris in 1997, "It's great fun, and he's got that band driving there and there's great electricity in the audience and everybody's up. It's fun to see him, only if it is for a minute or two." However, Regis admitted, "I don't like to be interviewed by David – I think it's a tough seat – but I don't mind going on his show and participating in whatever stunt he has available." Letterman's admiration was no soft soap. In the spring of 1994, it was widely believed that at his urging Philbin was being considered to host CBS's post-Letterman late-night entry. But once again Regis quickly offered a "Thanks, but no thanks" response by citing prior commitments. "I'm flattered to be considered," he was quoted as saying by *Entertainment Weekly* on April 22, 1994. "But I'm tied to my own show until 1995. And I don't think CBS will want to wait to cash in on Letterman's ratings."

Regis himself was willing to cash in on his popularity by signing a $1-million deal with Hyperion to write his memoirs. The lucky author would be *Esquire*'s Bill Zehme, who'd already proven himself to be a Philbin fanatic in articles written for the magazine. But Regis didn't want to write a typical autobiography of the kind Kathie Lee had written. He wanted something that was more in keeping with who he was and what his life was like. So, in *I'm Only One Man*, Regis via Zehme chronicles a year in the life of Philbin, using occasional flashbacks to fill the reader in on his early years. Notably absent from the book is much mention of his first wife, Kay Faylen, or even much mention of his two eldest children, which lent some credence to previously published stories that Regis wasn't a particularly hands-on father to Danny and Amy after he divorced their mother. However, every few pages Regis speaks lovingly of his current wife, Joy, and their life together. And she seems to reciprocate those affections, even when tattling on his more annoying qualities, such as his trouble with directions. "Regis doesn't always know where he's going," Joy told Zehme. "It's a character flaw, but nothing I can't live with."

While Philbin is reluctant to discuss his first wife, he takes every opportunity to express his undying pride in Joy. Never was that more apparent than when she landed her own syndicated talk show called *Haven*, which billed itself as the first weekly television series devoted entirely to home decorating. "It's very near and dear to my heart," Joy told Jess Cagle of *Entertainment Weekly* in April 1994. "Since we've been married, Regis and I have done about eight houses." Although not her first experience on a show – she cohosted Regis's Lifetime series – this was the first time she was on her own without her husband beside her. Nonetheless, he did show up on *Haven* just to let her know she couldn't get too far away from him.

Sometimes, of course, fame can be a drawback, especially when overzealous fans and companies looking for a quick buck begin scrutinizing one's earlier career, or so Philbin found out when Mercury Records reissued *It's Time for Regis!*, his long-out-of-print 1968 album of show tunes and standards. The press had a field day. *Entertainment Weekly*'s music reviewer Bob Cannon wrote, "Besides the thrill of his jaunty renditions of evergreens such as *Pennies From Heaven* and *Where or When*, you get *Swanee* done as a demented hybrid of Dixieland and Motown." Regis hoped that by not responding interest in the album would quickly fade, but his old boss, Joey Bishop, used the occasion to fire off a zinger at Regis, as quoted by Cannon. "I have to admit," he quipped, "his singing gives lots of hope to lots of people who can't sing."

Well, Philbin could let them laugh; he was too busy making trips to the bank. In addition to his autobiography, the performance appearances with and without Kathie Lee, his commercials, and the cookbooks, Regis was now a successful exercise video entrepreneur. *Regis Philbin: My Personal Workout* joined the crowded health video market, but Philbin thought he had a unique angle, as he mentioned in a press release. "Everybody's got a video, but almost no men!" he pointed out. "I'd always thought it was a woman's medium. What guy wants to see another guy doing exercises?"

At least that's what he thought before he had visions of his own mortality during his angioplasty scare the year before. After that, he made a serious commitment to live a healthier lifestyle. Not surprisingly, he attacked his new regime with his usual gusto. Radu Teodorescu, the Romanian-born trainer who starred in Cindy Crawford's two hot-selling fitness videos, said to Nanci Hellmich that Regis "has a very athletic background, very ball-game oriented – tennis, football, basketball. He played them. He enjoys them. He's very competitive, even with Cindy. If they meet in the gym, and we play some basketball, he's very competitive. Regis is fun to train, always he's got something cute to say, a word of wisdom."

Despite his love of game sports, Philbin admitted in a press release, "I'd worked out with weights all my life, but never exercised aerobically." He now power walks for half an hour three times a week. "I was not exercising my heart. I never jogged, walked or used a Stairmaster until I followed my doctor's orders last year and found out how much I'd been missing. Now I wish I could jump-start everybody!"

In an interview with Marion Long of the on-line service Homearts.com, Philbin went into greater detail. "I usually start off every workout with at least 20 to 25 minutes on the treadmill. I pump the thing up and walk for as long and as fast as I can." He admitted it wasn't until after his angioplasty that he got serious about aerobics. "I learned that you have to exercise your heart. That's where it all starts and ends. Forget about how big your arms are, it's how big your heart is, you know? I love to take a walk outdoors whenever I can – a walk in Central Park is great – but if I can't get outside, I have a treadmill at home."

What took even more discipline for Regis was changing his eating habits. "It has become a part of my life, trying to be careful about my diet. I used to eat a lot of meat; now I eat a lot of fish and chicken. But chicken is driving me crazy. How many times can you eat chicken before you want to kill yourself? I cannot eat another piece of chicken – I'm sorry! God! In New York, you're always eating out, and it's the same old menus all full of chicken dishes, and the Chef's Surprise. . . . So, in addition to the chicken and fish, I sometimes have a little slice of veal, or some ravioli – something that may not be the best nutritionally, but is not too bad. I've cut out butter; I've switched to skim milk; I wish I could cut out all the ice cream. I usually have fresh fruit, some kind of fruit salad, after my workout. I also use the workout as an excuse to drink more water. For some reason, in my younger days, I didn't believe in drinking water during a workout. But it really does help. I drink a bottle of it during each session."

Slowing down was more difficult for Philbin. He even began to take work-related vacations. As part of Fan Fair '94, Philbin and Gifford joined participating viewers for a five-day, four-night vacation at Walt Disney World by taking *Live! With Regis & Kathie Lee* on the road and taping it at the Orlando-based theme park. Not only did those who sprung for the vacation get to mingle with Regis and Kathie Lee, but they were also gifted with an autographed copy of the new cookbook, *Entertaining with Regis and Kathie Lee*, and Regis's fitness video.

From all appearances, the show was a well-oiled machine running at 100% efficiency. But beneath the gleaming surface was a dangerous undercurrent. Indicative of the ever-present tension was an incident on a show that May. The guest that day was James McDaniel, who plays Captain Arthur Fancy on NYPD Blue, one of ABC's biggest hits. But when Gifford discovered, on air, that the clip they'd be showing hadn't had the swear words beeped out, she glared at her producer and then took matters into her own hands. She apologized to her studio and television audience for what they'd be seeing. Regis, for once, seemed to be caught off guard and didn't really respond. However, McDaniel did. Incensed at Gifford's implication, he refused to go on the air, leaving producer Gelman with live television's worst nightmare: empty air time.

A couple of days after the incident, Regis made a telling comment on the show when he suggested that Kathie Lee and Gelman create a spin-off of the current show. "You two kids, who have had such a wonderful relationship lately, could have one show, and Regis could maybe have his own!" When asked a month later by *Entertainment Weekly*'s Jess Cagle about the incident, Gelman deflected the question. "I love babies, I love James McDaniel, I love Regis and Kathie Lee, I love my ponytail, and I just want everybody to be happy."

But Gifford was starting to make decidedly *un*happy noises. Almost from the beginning of the show's syndication, she'd dropped comments about quitting that never carried much bite. But in 1994 her words were more weighted. In an interview with Lawrence Eisenberg of *Good Housekeeping*, she admitted that her current success was "so much more than I ever dreamed it would be that you'd think: 'Is she never satisfied?' But I get bored easily, and I have to keep doing different things – growing. . . . After nine years, as wonderful as it's been, and as much as I adore Regis – and he and I will be friends forever – I feel like the old Peggy Lee song, 'Is That All There Is?' Maybe I'll find out that *Live! With Regis & Kathie Lee* is all I can do, but I'm not a frightened person."

Kathie Lee's musing coincided with negotiations of her contract, set to expire in August. Gifford told Eisenberg that there was only a 50% chance she'd resign, and even if she did it would only be for one year. She cited a couple of reasons for possibly leaving. First, she was hoping to star in a prime-time sitcom (which never materialized), and, second, she wanted to spend more time with her family. She admitted that Frank was often exasperated with her hectic schedule. "I think there are times when he feels neglected, and he has the right to feel that way," she mentioned to Eisenberg. "And I kind of feel neglected during football season. But what we have going for us is a real strong friendship, and a great love for each other, and a tremendous respect for each other's work that gets us through times like that."

When asked for his thoughts on the subject, Philbin was the ultimate diplomat, saying to Eisenberg he understood how Gifford felt. "I've done it for 11 years, nine with Kathie, and it's been terrific, but there's a sameness year after year after year. We'll have to say good-bye someday, and that's going to be a sad day for the two of us because it's been terrific."

But that time would not be then. Gifford did end up resigning, but only for one year, and with some conditions that had nothing to do with money. One issue was the affiliates' power to veto outside work. One incident that had Kathie Lee fuming was WABC's refusal to let her appear in an infomercial for Gary Smalley, a relationship counselor. She and Frank would have earned an easy $1 million to do a tape for his series called *Hidden Keys to Loving Relationships*. Kathie Lee had planned on giving the entire amount to charity but was thwarted when the affiliate thought the infomercials were "cheesy."

But the biggest deal breaker had to do with show content. Gifford was finally in a position of leverage and intended to use it against Gelman, and she wasn't shy about discussing her feelings with Jim Jerome of *Ladies Home Journal*. "We had some strongly worded discussions. They were trying to tell us our audience was dying to have the latest rap group and the host of *Studs* on. Let's see how Rosie Clooney's doing; let's bring on Tony Bennett. Why should we be like every other show? I didn't feel they had a better grasp of our audience than I did. I said I was going to leave if things didn't change." Obviously, Gifford had the upper hand and played it, though she was careful not to gloat. After the negotiations were finished, she simply said she and her producer now shared "an understanding and respect we didn't have there for a while." Although Regis had openly praised Gelman's ability to keep control of the show, he could only stand by and watch events unfold. He still had the utmost confidence in his producer, but he knew everyone had to find a way to coexist if the show were to continue.

But while all might have been temporarily quiet on the *Live! With Regis & Kathie Lee* front, soon Gifford's private life would become a matter of public display. In February 1995, Atrid Gifford, Frank's second wife, did an interview with *Hard Copy* in which she openly and bitterly accused Kathie Lee of being, if not an outright adulterer, then at least a home wrecker. "She kept calling the house right from the beginning, asking to borrow Frank as an escort," Astrid claimed. "Kathie was all hands over my husband." She also warned women watching that "there are piranhas out there."

Kathie Lee and Frank took a patronizing attitude to the incident in a statement to the press. "This kind of gossip is . . . practically ancient history," they said, reminding everyone they had now been married eight years. "We started our relationship with clear consciences, which we still have today. It's just so sad that others have not been able to get on with life and find the same happiness."

What made Regis happy was being liked and returning the feelings. He was able to accomplish both by going back to his roots, as it were. In 1995, his old Bronx school, Cardinal Hayes, needed help. The school that had once been predominantly Italian and Irish American was now almost 99% African American and Latino. The racial makeup of the school indicated in general that the students came from families more economically challenged than those when Regis attended. School officials estimated that about 40% of the 1,500 students couldn't afford the school's tuition and fees. As a result, the school faced an annual deficit of about $1 million. What made the situation even more dire was that the Archdiocese of New York announced that it would stop giving subsidies to all of the city's Catholic schools by 1997. To be able to educate the pupils, the administration at Cardinal Hayes High School established an endowment fund to replace subsidies received from the archdiocese. "We were warned that in 1997 the school would have to be independent of the archdiocese," says Joseph Valenti, director of development at Cardinal Hayes. "So we set up the fund."

When Philbin heard about the school's situation, he immediately opened his checkbook. "I've contributed about $10,000 to the school so far," he told Juliette Fairley of *Black Enterprise*. "Because even though the Bronx has changed since I was a student there, Hayes is still educating young men. That's why I do what I do for Hayes." Yet, in typical Regis style, once the school reached – and exceeded – its goal of raising $5 million, he mentioned it almost in passing on *Live! With Regis & Kathie Lee* despite having been one of the more active fund-raisers. It was just another example of how he was the polar opposite of his cohost, which meant that he was the ballast that kept the show from lilting into self-parody.

Newsday's Marvin Kitman essayed the state of the hosts by saying, "Kathie Lee's function on the show is to be the target. In the old days, Regis would remark on her nightclub act or what she looked like in a bikini. He made fun of her, and she said silly things. Sometimes she would get in a zinger. But that has changed. The reason the show is so successful now is that her greatest achievement is her obnoxiousness; talking about herself and her other achievements is the perfect foil to Regis. It pays off. Obnoxiousness *was* his stock in trade. His show was going nowhere until they found someone more obnoxious. Everybody now feels sorry for Regis' having to put up with Kathie Lee, at the same time he has to take all that money home every week."

Kitman's comments came when new rumors were swirling that once again Gifford was threatening to quit when her contract expired in August 1996. This time, the wisdom whisperers even had a replacement picked out: Vanna White. The story was so pervasive that even Regis brought it up on the air to Kathie Lee. She was typically coy when talking to columnist Liz Smith of *Newsday*. "My contract is up in August and I have been making year-to-year deals because I like to keep re-evaluating my obligations to my husband and my children. But I really haven't decided. . . . I hope to work things out and stay. There are obstacles to staying, but the big reason to do so is – Regis! He's the biggest plus. I can't imagine my life without him."

For Kitman, Vanna could never sit in Kathie Lee's chair. "If you subscribe to the obnoxiousness theory, it would be difficult to find a suitable replacement for Kathie Lee. . . . The only way Vanna could do it is if they held up cards with letters spelling out the banter."

But in what was becoming a yearly ritual, Gifford's "Will she or won't she renew?" imbroglio was making life at the show tense for everyone, especially Regis. One particularly unusual episode occurred after Gifford appeared as a guest on CNBC's *Charles Grodin Show*. Grodin asked her about her frequently aired complaints over guests to book, to which Gifford replied much the same way she usually did in interviews. "Michael Gelman started out as an intern, and he's very, very smart, but the problem I have is he thinks he understands the audience. He's a male Jewish single guy living in New York, and there's nothing wrong with that, God bless him. But most of our audience are mothers . . . and they're out there in middle America. I think I understand a little better the kinds of guests they want to see." Then she added for emphasis, "It's come down to a point where I will not re-sign for one more year unless my feelings are respected."

The next day, when promos for the show were sent out, Gifford's comments were included, almost causing Kathie Lee to combust spontaneously. She accused CNBC of improperly promoting her comments to the press, even claiming she never said what they'd taped her saying. CNBC responded with this statement: "In no way did the CNBC public relations department *ambush* Ms. Gifford. . . . We are sorry that she was embarrassed by her comments made on Mr. Grodin's program. But, she did in fact make those statements. . . . As for Ms. Gifford's statement that she will never appear on CNBC again, we concur." There must have been times Regis wished Kathie Lee would go off and find something to keep her happy and occupied so he could concentrate on making *Live! With Regis & Kathie Lee* the entertainment show he wanted it to be instead of an ongoing soap opera.

Of course, not everyone was upset at the prospect of Kathie Lee leaving the show. *Entertainment Weekly* reminded readers that *Washington Post* television critic Tom Shales noted, "I find her at least as frightening as Godzilla." But among the people who counted, the viewers, it was a different story, one that didn't bode well for Regis and the show. According to a poll conducted by the magazine, 55% of those who responded had favorable or very favorable opinions of Gifford. Asked if they thought the news media had been unfairly picking on her, only 31% said yes. But when asked whom they'd rather be stranded on an island with, Kathie Lee beat out Regis 44% to 15%.

More than once, Gifford commented that she signed one-year contract extensions because if Regis left the show for some reason she didn't want to be stuck doing it with anybody else. Indeed, the idea of the show without Regis as the leveler is almost incomprehensible. However, if Gifford were to leave, Philbin acknowledged he'd continue the show without her. Although he struck gold with Kathie Lee, he believed the show could survive, albeit not as well, without her. "If she decided she wanted out or wanted to go into a sitcom or whatever. . . . This is the only thing I know how to do," he told the *Minneapolis Star-Tribune*'s Curt Schleier. "The only thing I want to do is this kind of show. So unless I'm ready to retire, if you don't mind, I'd like to continue with my life." Aware that this issue had caused friction between them before, Philbin added, "She expects me to say 'If she goes, I go too.' Where am I gonna go? Look, we're crushing the opposition like a runaway beer truck. Why would I leave?"

In the fall of 1995, two days after cohosting the 75th Miss America Pageant, Kathie Lee announced she would no longer participate in the annual event. In a short statement released by Buena Vista Television, Gifford said, "I have been honored to be a part of the Miss America tradition. I congratulate the new Miss America, Shawntel Smith, and wish her a wonderful and rewarding year as well as all the young women across our country who participate in every level of competition."

Although no specific reason was given for her departure, many thought that Gifford was freeing up her schedule to devote time to her latest venture: her new clothing "collection" being marketed by Wal-Mart. The line actually wasn't her first dabble in the rag trade. The manufacturer Halmode had attached her name to its Plaza South label in 1992. This time around, the Kathie Lee Collection was aimed at a mass-market audience and featured jackets, skirts, pants, and blouses that when mixed and matched would cost only about $50. "I decided to go mass-market, because I wanted to be where America lives and shops," Gifford told Rochelle Chadakoff of *Newsday* while being chauffeured from the *Live! With Regis & Kathie Lee* studio back to her Connecticut home. Gifford went on to tell Chadakoff that Wal-Mart was the perfect company to be in business with and that the clothing line provided "a continual way to give to favorite charities," with approximately 10% of each purchase going to charities, including Paul Newman's Hole in the Wall Gang and facilities that the Giffords were helping to secure for crack-addicted babies and HIV-positive children.

But this business venture would become a public relations struggle for Kathie Lee. In April 1996, Charles Kernaghan, executive director of the National Labor Committee, addressed a gathering of House Democrats at a House Democratic Policy Committee meeting. Rep. George Miller, D-Calif., committee cochairman, used the session to urge consumers to step up pressure on U.S. manufacturers to adopt codes of conduct for foreign contractors and to police them. Kernaghan told the committee his group had gone "to see one of the plants in Honduras where Kathie Lee clothes are made and saw over 100 children in this plant making clothing." He described how children, most between the ages of 13 and 15, work for the "starvation wages" of 31¢ to 39¢ an hour from 8 a.m. to 9 p.m. Monday through Friday and from 8 a.m. to 5 p.m. on Saturdays. Holding up a pair of Kathie Lee slacks made in the Honduran factory, Kernaghan added: "We call on Kathie Lee to use her national prominence to say that never again will child labor be used to produce garments."

A 15-year-old Honduran named Wendy Diaz would later appeal publicly to Gifford. Speaking at a Capitol Hill news conference, Wendy described the appalling working conditions at the factory where she'd been employed for two years making Kathie Lee sportswear for U.S. retail giant Wal-Mart. She said she was among about 100 children, some as young as 12 years old, who routinely worked 60 hours a week for 31¢ an hour. She also claimed that the South Korean owners of the factory,

Global Fashion, threatened, physically abused, and sexually harassed their young workers.

The accusations exploded onto the airwaves. Immediately, Kathie Lee was on the defensive, in part because the topic of sweatshops wasn't completely uncharted territory. A spokesman for Gifford said she and the companies licensed to make and sell the successful Kathie Lee Collection of career sportswear, which tallied $250 million in sales in 1995, had severed all ties with the plant in Choloma, Honduras, once problems were discovered.

Later, spokesman Ron Konecky added in a press release, "Kathie Lee Gifford was totally unaware of any problem with the manufacturing of the Kathie Lee Gifford Collection at the Choloma, Honduras, plant or with any other vendor utilizing improper manufacturing practices, as Kathie Lee is not directly involved with the vendor selection." He also said, "When the problem in Honduras was brought to her attention, she immediately contacted Wal-Mart and was advised that the relationship with the Choloma plant had been severed. Kathie Lee Gifford formed her clothing line to benefit children and would never condone, tolerate, or accept the exploitation of children."

A Wal-Mart spokesman, Dale Ingram, assured people in another press release that Wal-Mart had a strict policy against buying from manufacturers who use child labor. "One strike and you're out."

In June, Gifford spoke to an estimated crowd of 20,000 at Wal-Mart's annual meeting in Fayetteville, Arkansas, and told them that concerns about sweatshop labor making her clothing line were largely overblown by the media. "The viciousness of it is overwhelming," Gifford said of the news coverage. "Of course, we are appalled if any child is exploited or abused, but the thing is, we didn't do anything wrong. None of us knew it was happening." She also said she knew people would be skeptical about her profits from the line and a decision to donate some proceeds to charities. "The minute I realized how success-ful this line was, I knew the honeymoon was over. They told me that nobody would believe that we made it honestly."

Wal-Mart executives also attributed recent attacks over the use of international and domestic sweatshops to Wal-Mart's continued success as a discount retailer. "Five years ago, there was no bad story written about Wal-Mart, and now everybody wants to take a shot at us," spokesman Jay Allen said at a press conference after the meeting. "Any time a company or indi-vidual is successful, there is a small number of people out there who are determined to bring you down." Nonetheless, he noted, "We are a great company. We have 60 million customers a week in our stores, and they love Kathie Lee."

Lee Scott, executive vice president for merchandising, said Wal-Mart had upgraded its inspections at plants where company merchandise was manufactured. "We are doing everything humanly possible," said Scott, who also took the opportunity of the meeting to unveil a new line of Kathie Lee Gifford hair curlers and a hair dryer to the cheering crowd of investors and employees.

However, others weren't so convinced that Wal-Mart was as upstanding as it presented itself. An editorial by Eyal Press in the *Progressive* noted, "While the *entertainer who just had a simple idea* claims to be supporting needy children, only 10 per-cent of proceeds from sales goes to the kids. Dividing the rest between herself and Wal-Mart, Gifford predictably blames the sweatshop controversy on *that little cockroach down the line* – the small subcontracting shop that abuses workers behind the parent company's back. The truth is not so flattering. The gar-ment industry is by nature pyramidal, with real power in the hands of the big chains that set prices." Press went on to quote Neil Kearney of the International Textile, Garment, and Leather Workers Federation: "These companies adopt codes of conduct, some of them in very nice language, but then they negotiate deals which make it impossible for their contractors to honor the codes. The companies say to the contractor, 'Please allow for freedom of association, pay a decent wage,' but then they say, 'we will pay you eighty-seven cents to produce each shirt.' This includes the wage, fabric, everything."

Regardless of how much Wal-Mart executives truly knew, it was unfair to single out Gifford, just one among many celebrities who endorse clothing and shoe lines. And, to her credit, instead of trying to hide, she turned the situation to her advantage by taking a stand against the abuses of sweatshops and child labor. Speaking before the House International Relations subcommittee, she said, "it was nothing less than an assault on my very soul when a witness before Congress suggested that I was using the sweat of children to help children." By mid-July, leaders in Congress, along with Labor Secretary Robert Reich, the moderator at the Fashion Forum, were lauding Gifford as a selfless martyr who'd done more to focus public attention on child labor and sweatshops than anyone in memory.

Of course, there were those who thought Gifford had merely been visited by the karma fairy. Others, such as David Letterman, found humor in the situation, though his jokes at her expense put him on her hit list. "I thought he was a friend," she said. "In all the years I've been on television, I have never knocked anyone who's been having a tough time."

While it seemed that Gifford had weathered the storm, her halo had been knocked askew, and a patina of guilt by association remained. Suddenly, she was perhaps someone better left alone. That reality came into focus when it was announced that Regis would host that year's Miss America Pageant alone. When asked by the press if pageant officials would welcome Gifford back should she change her mind, a spokesman said brusquely, "That's too hypothetical. I'm not going to touch that. . . . She took herself out of it. She made an assessment a couple days later that she didn't want to do it anymore."

Also worrisome to Gifford was a *TV Guide* phone-in poll that concluded she was suffering major fallout. Of those who responded, 58% said they'd lost respect for her in light of the sweatshop scandal and believed *Live! With Regis & Kathie Lee* would be better off without her. A separate poll asked viewers whom they'd like to see replace her, and the resounding victor was none other than Joy Philbin. Although *TV Guide* managing editor Jack Curry told the press that "What we found in this survey is that people are sick of her," the show's syndicator, Buena Vista Television, said in a prepared statement that "we look forward to laughing with her in the morning for many years to come."

While Kathie Lee took a major image hit, Regis just kept rolling along, his iconic status solidifying with every sling and arrow aimed at his costar. "I try to be compassionate to Kathie Lee," he told Alex Witchel of the *Minneapolis Star Tribune*. "She's a lightning rod. I have to feel for her. Honestly, how is she supposed to know the labor situation in a factory in Honduras?" But, he acknowledged, "Yes, we're joined at the hip for that one hour, there's no doubt about it. What happens to her becomes the point of the show."

Interestingly, though Frank Gifford was frequently quoted defending his wife, Philbin chose largely to remove himself from the fray and concentrate on keeping the show on course, especially since he agreed to a multimillion-dollar contract that tied him to the show at least through the year 2000. Prior to the extension, Philbin was already earning a salary in the low millions, according to trade paper reports, but his new deal upped the amount considerably. So, if there was any doubt in anyone's mind whether or not Regis would continue the show should Gifford decide to bolt, his new contract spoke volumes.

Regis just wanted to let the good times roll. But he should have remembered that the greater the highs, the farther the fall.

8

Troubles with Kathie Lee

Musing over his 30-plus years in television, Regis Philbin admitted to Curt Schleier of the *Minneapolis Star Tribune*, "When I went into this business, I asked myself, 'People can sing and dance, and they're stand-up comedians. What have you got?'" His answer was, "I did have that ability to make other guys laugh, to pick up on something they said and work it to death. But that was the only thing I had." Yet it was enough to forge a career for Philbin.

After having been a talk show host for more than three decades, and the past eight years with Kathie Lee, Regis mentioned to Paul Harris in 1997 that he worried sometimes "I'm a little too casual about this because, frankly, we're on the air and sometimes I even forget we're on the air. I just start talking to her and to the camera, and I've got to be more attentive, I guess. But I've always thought that that was a special place and I wanted to keep it that way, which is why we really don't talk at all before the show starts."

Philbin acknowledged that at times the host chat segment threatened to take over the show, and he had to be careful about that. "Sometimes we go twenty-five minutes, and that's more than half the show, counting the commercials. And Gelman has got his two or three guests that he's got to get on, so he's having a fit. Twenty-five minutes is really enough of us and then we've got to start moving on to other things."

Off camera, Philbin's son, Danny, was moving in a new direction: marriage to a lawyer named Lila Bakke. Danny told Ann Oldenburg of USA Today the story of how his fiancée found out who his father was. "We were talking about our families," he related. "I said, 'You know that show Regis and Kathie Lee?' And she said, 'I hate that show.' And I said, 'That's my dad.'"

However, in typical fashion, Philbin's participation in the couple's rehearsal dinner – Regis was Danny's best man – didn't go exactly as planned. "I was in Chicago trying to segue to Milwaukee and we were met by the airline representative . . . who said, 'You have an hour to kill, so why don't we put you in the lounge?'" he related to Paul Harris in December 1997 in an online interview. "So I ended up there, and sure enough, the plane took off without us. Can you believe it? I could not believe it. The woman said, 'Guess what? The plane has left. What?!? You put me in the lounge and the plane left? Leave me alone!' I didn't know there was a lounge in the first place. Then they pick you up in one of those carts with the *beep beep beep beep*, and everyone is looking to see who it is. It's embarrassing. I mean, I was so bugged, because I was trying to get to his wedding rehearsal. That meant I had to rent a car and drive up there. So I missed the rehearsal all together, but I got there in time for the dinner." After his tirade, Philbin did note, "They're just trying to help you and, well, that was a once in a lifetime situation."

Regis also spent Thanksgiving with his son and new daughter-in-law that year, and it seemed that their deepening relationship was reflected in Philbin's becoming more vocal in promoting causes for the disabled. Regis accepted the emceeing chores for the National Rehabilitation Awareness Foundation's achievement awards and told the audience, "We're trying to make everyone more aware of the tremendous accomplishments of these people. One guy climbed a mountain with only the use of his arms!" But it wasn't only his son's plight that spurred Regis; he also had a cousin who'd lost his legs, in his case because of a car accident.

When speaking on such occasions, Regis spoke more openly about his son, proudly telling those in attendance that after 65 operations Danny was a miraculous success story. "He's overcome a lot," Philbin said with emotion to Ann Oldenburg. "He's got a great job, he's got a master's degree from Catholic University." And, after years of familial turmoil, it also seemed that Danny had the relationship with his father he'd always wanted.

Kathie Lee Gifford was slowly developing her own relationship with *Live! With Regis & Kathie Lee.* Her latest contract guaranteed her four-day workweeks during nonsweeps times. So, starting in 1997, she sat beside Regis only Monday through Thursday during the off-peak ratings times such as in December and January. Regis joked that she could have taken Thursday off as well. Perhaps he was only half joking, because 1997 was more trying than the previous year, which had been marred by the sweatshop scandal. Once again Kathie Lee was caught in the media crosshairs – this time as the wronged woman.

If there was one presiding thing about Kathie Lee that annoyed her critics, both in the media and in the audience, it was her unrealistic portrait of her married life with Frank – a portrait that most people instinctively knew was too perfect to be real. It wasn't even so much what she said as the *righteous* way she said it. So, in some ways, she set herself up for the vitriol that followed, an onslaught that made Regis wonder if the show would sink under the weight of the turmoil.

In mid-May, 1997, the *Globe* tabloid claimed that 66-year-old Frank Gifford had had an affair with a 46-year-old woman in a New York hotel just after having had lunch with Kathie Lee. The story broke the week Kathie Lee was to give a commencement address at Marymount University. Predictably, she immediately and vehemently labeled the story a lie and used the occasion to tell the graduates, "we live in a cash for trash age." She kept calling the story a lie until the *Globe* countered by publishing 10 photos of Frank and his blonde lover pawing each other, on not just one but two occasions. Making the story more tawdry was the revelation that the *Globe* had placed a video camera in the room and had paid the woman, Suzen Johnson, $75,000 to set up a rendezvous with Frank. She told the tabloid Frank had been pursuing her hot and heavy for four years.

Tony Frost, the editor of the *Globe*, said he'd refrained from publishing the photos at first and was only doing so then because the Giffords contended that the earlier story of Frank's affair with the flight attendant was a lie. In the May 23, 1997, issue publishing the photos, the *Globe* noted, "Ironically, the Catholic school, which campaigns against sweatshop abuses, honored Kathie Lee even though she was lambasted because her clothing line was made by Honduran kids working 20-hour days." So, the *Globe* said, it was "forced to print these revealing photos to prove to the 43-year-old *Live* hostess that her cheating husband is the one not telling the truth." Perhaps the most humiliating aspect was that excerpts from their bedroom talk were also published, including Frank's complaints that there were certain things his wife refused to do sexually that he wanted the willing Johnson to do.

For once Kathie Lee didn't have a comeback. Instead, through a representative, she and Frank asked that people respect their privacy while they worked the matter out between them. "This experience has been as painful for us as it would be for any other couple," they said in a joint statement. "However, we will get through this together." And for once Gifford had little to say on *Live! With Regis & Kathie Lee* about her life at home, making no mention of the matter, though the tension in the air was palpable to anyone watching. Kathie Lee had the faraway look of someone on Prozac, and Regis gamely acted as if she was hearing his shtick and observations. He knew the show had become a hit mainly because it entertained people. Even his jousting with Gifford made people smile and feel better before going about their business. While a certain number of viewers would empathize with Kathie Lee, if the show became too "heavy" it would lose its charm and begin to lose its hold on viewers. All Regis could do was keep his own energy up and ride out the emotional tidal wave sure to follow.

Despite Kathie Lee's belief that all critics were out to get her, many wrote thoughtful pieces about her private situation gone so public. "The Giffords have been turned into instant water cooler gossip fodder, and America cannot seem to think of two more worthy subjects," observed Tom Long of *Gannett News Service* in a lengthy essay. "And make no mistake, these are two people who have set themselves up to hit the ground hard. Kathie Lee . . . for years has been proclaiming her golden relationship with Frank. She literally has told millions about . . . her devoted football star-turned-sports-announcer husband, about the ideal life they all lead. And Frank himself has pretty much been a poster boy for American jockism all his life, spouting the virtues of hard work and dedication for nearly three decades as the one steady host of *Monday Night Football*. Between them the couple had become the entertainment equivalent of Jim and Tammy Faye Bakker."

Long went on to say that Gifford had become the female version of John Tesh, describing them both as "moderately talented, nice-looking entertainers whom a lot of people like and a whole lot of people hate for no good reason other than they personify – in their detractors' minds – the blandest level of American culture." But the difference between Gifford and

Tesh is that he didn't "push his swell life on the public near[ly] as much as Kathie Lee." Yet Long's point was that the sense of "You reap what you sow" was tempered by the fact that Frank had apparently been set up. Yes, he had succumbed, but having a camera waiting for him in that hotel room wasn't really playing fair.

The *Globe*'s involvement in the scandal generated a firestorm of media controversy perhaps summed up best by William Powers in the *New Republic*. Powers first burst the bubble of "legitimate" journalism by pointing out the hypocrisy by which pundits operate. They decry the tabloids, but in doing so they reproduce the sordid story in its entirety. In other words, they get to retell the story while ostensibly maintaining their journalistic integrity. "And so another juicy story paid for by the tabs passes into the mainstream press – for free." To Powers, that was hypocrisy of the worst kind.

He then went on to explain the great myth of tabloids – that, because their methods might be unscrupulous, so are their messages. "In fact, as the Frank Gifford story demonstrates, the supermarket weeklies are the unlikely tribunes of an exacting moral code, a set of rules that reflects how most Americans think about the world much more faithfully than does the minimalist moral system that informs the coverage of the big media outlets," Powers asserted. "Undergirding all tabloid journalism is a rigid code of right and wrong, in which people are held to very particular standards of behavior. In this system, which may be the closest thing we have today to a universal populist ethos, all the ancient social norms are honored: thou shalt not kill, rape, steal, lie and so forth."

The way Powers saw it, the biggest sins are pride and hypocrisy and phoniness, which is why Kathie Lee was so clearly a target, just as the O.J. Simpson story was, which, Powers pointed out, "was not a parable about race, as the mainstream media suggested. It was about a celebrity who thought he was above the law. . . . Which brings us back to Frank Gifford and, more importantly, to his wife, Kathie Lee. There is something about Kathie Lee Gifford that seems to drive a lot of people crazy, a chirpy perkiness suspect for its degree and its ubiquity that violates the tabloids' cardinal rule: no phoniness."

And that seemed to be the crux for the tittering reaction to the Giffords' marriage troubles, as the *People* mailbag seemed to echo. "Kathie Lee Gifford's 'business as usual' demeanor is insulting given that she has made the most intimate details of her life a part of millions of people's morning routine," wrote Andrea H. Dumas. "There seemed nothing too personal or too vulgar to mention on television. Now that what is revealed is unflattering and humiliating, Kathie Lee needs her privacy. Well, if she hadn't shoved Frank and her 'perfect marriage' down our throats for the better part of a decade, maybe we wouldn't care."

Another writer, Peggy Deutsch, fumed, "Our daughter graduated from Marymount University, and I had high hopes for a special message to the graduates from Kathie Lee. There is no question that her address was fierce, but her remarks were entirely self-centered and self-serving. Every statement related to her good works and unfair treatment by the 'trash for cash' press. It was an infomercial, not a commencement address."

Then there were the cynics, such as J. Stanton, who noted, "Let's hope this image-conscious couple decide to handle this unseemly affair privately and not plan a moneymaking deal with marriage counselor Gary Smalley, with new self-help videotapes and books just in time for Christmas!"

The Gifford-Johnson-Kathie Lee brouhaha would remain on the front pages of the tabloids for the rest of the year, forcing Regis to grin and bear it. He said nothing when Kathie Lee brought along a bodyguard instead of Frank to Hawaii for a week's taping of *Live! With Regis & Kathie Lee.* He teased her less than he might otherwise have when she began an obvious makeover, cutting her hair, losing significant weight, and wearing more sexy clothes on the show. While shooting in Hawaii, she sported a hot pink bikini and flirted openly with her bodyguard (nobody was sure why she needed a bodyguard in the first place).

However, even if viewers didn't know what to expect from Gifford when they tuned in every morning, they figured that Regis would be the same old Regis. Yet the wear and tear would occasionally show on Philbin, who'd say later to Paul Harris, "It was tough. The flack was really flying and the television tabloid shows were coming around. It wasn't easy to get through that, and there were some mornings where I just hated it, but you just have to go on the air with it." When Harris asked if there were some mornings when Kathie Lee asked Regis to steer clear, he responded, "Listen, we know each other so well now – I think it's been twelve years since we've been together – that I know what to bring up and she does too, and what not to bring up. Naturally, we weren't going to talk about that situation on our show."

What Philbin tried to do, he told Alex Witchel of the *Minneapolis Star Tribune*, was, regardless of Gifford's trauma of the day, "keep it small. This is a notorious business for burning out fast," he said. "I'm with you every morning, we're having our coffee; you're having yours. There's nothing urgent about the show. It's just time together." Philbin was well aware, though, that he saw the time spent on the show differently than his costar did. "Because of the tough times, she's a little more sensitive," he told David Bauder of Associated Press. "You've got to watch what you're saying. You don't want to embarrass her. But I've got to tell you something – she's a fighter."

Even though Regis avoided getting directly involved on air, to some he couldn't help but be tainted by mere proximity. Coincidentally or not, he wasn't asked to host the 1997 Miss America Pageant. Instead, executive producer Leonard Horn made the surprising announcement at a press conference that emceeing duties were being assigned to *All My Children* stars – and married couple – John and Eva LaRue Callahan. "I thought he [Regis] did a terrific job," said Horn. "But ABC felt we would have a better chance at attracting a younger audience with John and Eva." Eva admitted to Mary Green and Terry Kelleher of *People* that she and John were "shocked" when asked. But, John added, "Once the shock wore off, I said, 'We do a lot together, so why not this?'"

Philbin concurred that the change most likely had to do with network – not Gifford – affiliation. "I'll tell you what happened," he explained to Paul Harris. "I did it for, I think, four or five years with Kathie Lee, and then I did it alone last year. But we've had a change in the network. ABC is carrying the show this year, not NBC, and they wanted to go with a younger, hipper, funnier, better looking version of Regis, so they wound up with this husband and wife team from *All My Children*. I just interviewed the lady a couple of weeks ago. A very, very nice and good looking gal, Eva Larue Callahan."

However, what made the hiring of Eva and John unusual was that the previous month she'd been written out of the soap after her character, Maria, disappeared in a plane crash, a plot twist that enabled Eva to move on to *Head over Heels*, a new fall sitcom on rival weblet UPN.

Philbin said to Harris that he couldn't disagree with ABC's thinking. "You'd be surprised that those soap opera stars have a big following." Then he added, "I did it, I was there, it was a lot of fun, and frankly it was all a lot of work, and I've moved on to bigger and better things." After a second, he brought up the fact that he wouldn't be there the first year bikinis were allowed and said in his put-upon-guy voice, "Yeah, darn it, just when they get bikinis, I have to leave. There you go. . . . If they remove any more clothing, it becomes a pay-per-view event!"

Although Regis kept up his usual upbeat persona in public,

on the set of *Live! With Regis & Kathie Lee* apathy was beginning to set in. Now, instead of mingling with the audience after the show to sign autographs or have his picture taken, Regis had a page inform audience members to leave the item to be auto-graphed at the reception desk, where they could "retrieve" it after the show. During an interview with Ed Bark of the *Dallas Morning News* in November 1997, Michael Gelman was apa-thetic to the point of narcosis. "Executive producer Michael Gelman and his decidedly deadpan demeanor arrive six min-utes before air time," wrote Bark. "Summoning the enthusiasm of a tollbooth operator making change, he grudgingly lays out the basics. 'You bring life to the show. You bring energy to the show. You bring excitement to the show.' Zzz." Bark reported that at first Regis was the amicable host until he was given the wrong name for guest Laura San Giacomo's character on the NBC sitcom *Just Shoot Me*. Gelman's response was a mocking "Yeah, terrible mistake," at which point Philbin turned away from his producer and the audience in an apparent huff. Bark ended the piece by recounting how Regis "reprimands a young, green publicist for failing to treat him with the proper defer-ence," prompting Bark to conclude, "Disney ownership or no, this is not the happiest place on Earth."

Regis's less jovial side was also apparent that Christmas season when he took on the beloved Elmo. That was the winter of the Tickle-Me Elmo mania, generated in part by Rosie O'Donnell's fascination with the chuckling plush toy. After Regis spoke ill of the toy on *Live! With Regis & Kathie Lee* by saying "I hate Elmo," the Children's Television Workshop, which produces *Sesame Street*, backed out of a planned visit to the show, on which Elmo was scheduled to sing. According to a statement released by CTW, "Elmo would be very uncomfort-able." Producer Gelman was unmoved, saying to Mark Potok of *USA Today* that CTW should "lighten up." In response, CTW noted, "We are big fans of Regis and Kathie Lee. . . . And we wish Gelman a very merry Christmas."

What made the incident notable is that, while Regis has always been excitable and opinionated, like Don Rickles he is seldom mean-spirited. It seemed as if he just wanted to do the show without all the outside traumas. But as long as he was partnered with Kathie Lee, that seemed to be impossible. If she wasn't embroiled in some battle with the media or emoting about saving her marriage, it was the guessing game of whether she would or would not be back for another year. As 1997 wound down, Regis wondered once again who his cohost would be a year from then.

Gifford still talked about starring in a prime-time sitcom, but that was unlikely given the sweatshop scandal and the Frank-Johnson affair. And she fancied herself a singer in demand, so there was always that career route to take. However, when reviewing her CBS Christmas special, the *Washington Post*'s Tom Shales, as quoted by Norm Clarke, wrote, "Kathie Lee Gifford sings songs like she's mad at them. . . . You'd think she would be intent on getting back at her husband rather than taking it out on us."

Even if Regis wanted her to quit just to bring peace back to the workplace, Kathie Lee would be a tough act to replace. With her in the cohost's chair, *Live! With Regis & Kathie Lee* was still a dominant daytime show. The most recent sweeps rating was a solid 4.5 – up from a 4.2 the previous November, according to Nielsen data. In New York, the ratings were even stronger, though they'd gone down a fraction (a 6.3 in 1997 compared with a 6.7 in November 1996), but the show still easily won its 9-10 a.m. time slot on WABC, channel 7. For her efforts, Gifford was compensated a reported $3-5 million annually.

Although a spokeswoman for Disney-owned Buena Vista Television, which produces the show, said in a press release,

"Everything's the same; she reviews her contract a year at a time and it's not time for a decision now," for Regis it was very much an issue because, if she did leave, picking her replacement would be of primary importance for the show to remain successful.

Despite his longevity and the daily dose of admiration from the audience and fans, Regis probably wasn't sure at that moment if he had the fan support to carry the show on his own. All performers have that sliver of doubt. In a year's time, though, Philbin would find out just how capable he was of drawing a large audience on his own.

9

A New Mountain to Climb

When someone with his fingers so firmly on the pulse of pop culture as Jerry Seinfeld wants you on his show, you don't say no. That's how Regis and Kathie Lee came to appear in *Seinfeld*'s fifth-season finale, featuring the character Kramer on *Live! With Regis & Kathie Lee* plugging his coffee table book. But Philbin admitted he occasionally cringes when he sees it air in reruns. According to a newswire service, Seinfeld insisted Philbin repeatedly exclaim, "This guy is bonkos!" Regis wryly recalled, "Jerry insisted that people would scream with laughter if I said *bonkos*. Let me tell you, he was wrong."

But there wasn't much wrong Regis could do. Everywhere he went, he left good feelings in his wake and gained even more fans. While filming *Live! With Regis & Kathie Lee* at Mount Rushmore, he endeared himself to local residents by climbing to the top of the granite sculpture while Gifford took a swing by via helicopter. "That's the story of our life," Regis later noted at a press conference. "I climbed, and she flew up in a helicopter with a cup of tea."

If there was one drawback to being part of such a popular duo, it was that people usually wanted to see Regis with Kathie Lee. So, when *Diagnosis Murder* called, it was not for Regis but for Regis and Kathie Lee. The Dick Van Dyke vehicle had taken a page from *Murder, She Wrote* and become a haven for clever guest casting, such as having Mike Connors appear as Mannix and Barbara Bain as her *Mission: Impossible* character. In keeping with their tongue-in-cheek approach to cameos, the writers scribed a screenplay in which Regis and Kathie Lee play, of all things, talk show hosts and in which Philbin "accidentally" murders Gifford. (In a trivia footnote, that *Diagnosis Murder* episode was the final film appearance of Mary Frann, who costarred with Bob Newhart on the long-running series *Newhart* and died later in the autumn of 1998.) Although Regis and Kathie Lee were role playing, some critics half-jokingly wondered if the *Diagnosis Murder* appearance was cathartic. As the *Rocky Mountain News* of Denver wrote, "On tonight's episode of *Diagnosis Murder*, Regis Philbin shoots Kathie Lee Gifford. Not only that – for this episode they're changing the show's title to *Diagnosis Justifiable Homicide*."

All levity aside, though, more than one reviewer noted how the atmosphere of *Live! With Regis & Kathie Lee* seemed to be increasingly strained. Or, as Ken Tucker of *Entertainment Weekly* put it, the show had "taken on the sweaty, embattled atmosphere of what I imagine it was like being trapped along with Patricia Hearst when she was kidnapped by the Symbionese Liberation Army." Except, instead of political revolutionaries, the once-happy morning show had Gifford giving "us screeds about proper child rearing and the venality of a free press. Meanwhile, long-suffering, increasingly exhausted-looking Regis Philbin watches in misery."

Philbin himself acknowledged a similar sentiment on occasion with his well-worn joke, "Once I didn't talk to her for two weeks. . . . I didn't want to interrupt her."

Although the show still pulled in strong ratings, Regis and Kathie Lee were no longer the newest kids on the daytime talk show block. That distinction now belonged to another ABC show, *The View*, the brainchild of Barbara Walters, coproducer as well as cohost. Her idea could be seen as an extended and updated version of Philbin's host chat (itself an extended and updated version of Jack Paar's opening chat with his audience). Joining Walters on *The View* were Debbie Matenopoulos, Star Jones, Joy Behar, and Meredith Vieira, though Matenopoulos would later leave. The opening segment of *The View* consisted of 20 minutes of chat and banter between the cohosts – much of it pointed. It wasn't so much happy talk as it was sassy talk. And, for some reason, it had daytime TV all abuzz.

"We're not trying to change the face of daytime," averred coproducer Bill Geddie at a press conference. "We just want viewers to have a strong alternative. This is a talk show where people actually talk and do not fight. We treat guests with respect. And the audience is growing."

At press interviews, Vieira said the show is completely Barbara's. "Barbara packaged it, sold the network on the concept and won't stint on the concept. She has argued the case for a little intelligence at this time of the morning. She didn't want happy talk and she didn't want boring. She felt the concept of four diverse women who had things on their minds would attract viewers." Vieira summed up the show's appeal by saying, "We're the thinking woman's alternative. But it's perfectly all right if men sneak a peek, too."

While *The View* was making waves with its combination of free-flow chat and topics of the day, Regis refused to change or let the competition cause him to adjust his style in any way. "We're just trying to give them a few laughs," he said of his audience at a press conference, and he'd continue to do so the best way he knew how. Even still, watching *The View* brought into sharp focus how much the general atmosphere of *Live! With Regis & Kathie Lee* had changed since Gifford's early days. But Regis was Regis. *Newsweek* included him in its list of "TV People Who Create Buzz," along with the likes of *Today* producer Jeff

Zucker, MSNBC's Don Imus, and fellow talk show hosts Rosie O'Donnell and Oprah Winfrey.

Regis and Kathie Lee made history, of a sort, when they became the first "real people" to appear on *The Simpsons*. In the episode, Lisa and Bart interact with the real-life hosts after the kids are zapped into their TV while being chased by a homicidal Itchy and Scratchy. Jerry Springer and Ed McMahon also appear on the show, but only as cartoon characters.

As 1998 rolled into 1999, the world turned its attention to the approaching millennium, and Regis faced another year wondering if it would be his last with Kathie Lee, who continued to make noises about leaving the show for good once her contract expired. But the two hosts had stopped discussing such matters, and Philbin acknowledged at a press interview, "Every day – this does start to wear you down." That was one reason he was always on the lookout for a new challenge, a new adventure, a new creative mountain to climb. And, in the early months of 1999, he found what would prove to be his personal Everest.

Regis got wind that ABC was developing a new game show based on a hit British series. He looked into it, he admitted to Jess Cagle of *Entertainment Weekly* in November 1999, at Joy's prodding. "*Live* is over at 10 o'clock and by 1:30, I'm home." Joy explained to Cagle that "We need to have separate time, so I said, 'You really need an afternoon job.'" Regis translated that as "Why don't you find something to do?" He'd considered game shows before. Because it was a genre in which he'd already failed twice, and being as competitive as ever, Regis wanted to give it another shot. But he'd turned down many game shows over the years, so it would have to be the *right* show. And if it were, he thought, "it might be something to kill, say, one afternoon a week," he said at a press conference.

What began as a nice idea became an obsession after tapes of the British version of *Who Wants to Be a Millionaire?* landed on his desk. "I wanted it!" he exclaimed to reporters. "This is the first one that's come along that really caught my eye," he said. "I loved the production values. I wanted to be a part of it." But to his surprise, neither the network nor the show's producer showed much interest in having him be the show's host. "My name was not on the list, thank you very much." That's all Regis needed to hear. He began a strategic campaign to be hired as the host via phone calls and string pulling. "I had to pitch myself!" Regis fumed in his Philbinesque way. And what was his pitch? "Forget Bill Cullen! I'm here! Some of these guys on the list are dead fourteen years. And ahead of Regis! And here I am knocking myself out all these years."

On a more serious note, he said, "I have never felt that I was high on ABC's priority list for anything. And yes, I could have said, 'You don't want me, I don't want you.' I guess I was hurt a little bit. But I got over it. I had to get on the phone and say, 'Look, I'm turning down a lot of shows, but this is the one that really knocks me out. It's the most compelling television I've seen in years. I'd love to be considered for it. I really love this show.' When you do something every day, year after year, you yearn for something different," he added.

Producer Michael Davies's recollection is that Philbin *was* on the shortlist, along with Bob Costas, Phil Donahue, and Montel Williams, but Philbin's enthusiasm far exceeded anyone else's. "He blew me away with both his passion for the program and his understanding of the format," Davies said. "He pledged that he'd do anything to be considered: audition, travel to London, anything. He really wanted it. So I thanked him, hung up the phone, and instantly crossed out the other names on the list."

One of the first things Regis did was fly to England to watch a taping of the show. He saw a surprisingly intense program in which everyday people had a chance to win the money of their dreams. The British host was rather staid but tortured contestants by asking them "Is that your final answer?" in such a taunting way as to make them think they were wrong. Or, as Ken Tucker of *Entertainment Weekly* observed, "The host of the Brit edition, Chris Tarrant, favors black suits, black shirts, black ties, and affects a vaguely sinister demeanor when he asks a contestant, 'Is that your final answer?' – as if a 'Yes' followed by a mistake might result in the floor opening up and the poor sod plummeting down into the fires of hell." Michael Davies added at a press interview, "Philbin is very much on the side of the contestant; Tarrant will absolutely torture them." He also noted Philbin understands that the "host has to play a remarkably fine line between being the contestant's best friend and playing the slightly mischievous angle."

It had been a long time since a game show had aired in prime time, and the executives at ABC knew it was a gamble, but at that point, as the third-place network, it had little to lose. While game shows have been a staple of daytime programming nearly since the invention of television, the genre has fallen out of favor for a variety of reasons over the years. Game shows were at their peak of popularity in the 1950s when the big-money quiz show ruled the prime-time airwaves, beginning with the June 1955 debut of CBS's *The $64,000 Question*. The idea was to create "spectacle television." To add drama for viewers, the format was constructed so that contestants answered questions only in their field of expertise. This way, questions that were moderately difficult for contestants were unimaginably hard for viewers, giving them the feeling that they were watching geniuses. The element that heightened the drama was the risk factor – chancing the loss of what you had for an even bigger pot of gold.

In an effort to match the popularity and inherent drama of *The $64,000 Question*, a producer of the rival show *Twenty-One*, Dan Enright, rigged his game show. He figured that, if he supplied certain answers to certain contestants, he could make underdogs into superstars, boosting the ratings in the process. The scheme worked. The first such manufactured celebrity created as a *Twenty-One* contestant was Herbert Stempel. But Stempel was quickly dismissed in favor of the handsome and charming Charles Van Doren. Whereas Stempel had become an "everyman" hero, Van Doren was the stuff of golden celebrity and quickly became a national phenomenon, which prompted *Time* to put him on one of its covers. But as television would demonstrate many times over the years, nobody likes to lose. So, feeling slighted and cheated, Stempel blew the whistle on Enright by going public with the rigging.

The fallout was immediate and disastrous. Even though there was no specific governing body that made cheating technically illegal, it was seen as morally reprehensible by the 1950s public. With headlines blaring "*Twenty-One* Fixed!" the golden age of game shows soon came to an inglorious end, and by the end of the decade quiz shows had disappeared from prime-time television.

The next generation of quiz shows was quite different in tone and procedure. More elements of chance were introduced, and the rules became complicated. As a result, game shows lost both popularity and prestige and became relegated to daytime programming. But during that time, they slowly regained some of their sheen. Producers such as Mark Goodson and Bill Todman created game shows such as *Password*, *Family Feud*, and *The Price Is Right*. Then came Bob Stewart's *$10,000/ $25,000 Pyramid* followed by Merv Griffin, whose *Wheel of Fortune* and *Jeopardy!* helped to invigorate the genre and bring back some of its cachet, particularly thanks to *Wheel of Fortune*'s pairing of Pat Sajak and Vanna White.

Even though Griffin's game shows were still ratings getters, they symbolized what was wrong with game shows – there weren't any new ones being developed. In recent years, the only game shows to be produced are remakes of old shows, such as

Hollywood Squares and *Family Feud*. Instead, producers devoted their resources to talk shows that were equally cheap to produce and for a while drew big ratings. The problem with talk shows, to many minds, was that they had to become more and more outrageous to be competitive. Plus, so many shows were produced that the syndicated and local affiliate markets were saturated with them. It was the perfect time to go in a new direction.

One visionary who saw the public's weariness with talk shows as an opportunity was transplanted Englishman Michael Davies, ABC's executive vice president of alternative series and specials. As he said to reporters, "Literally, two days after *Millionaire* aired in England, I received eight copies of it, from my mother, my brother, and friends of mine in the television business. I watched it and instantly knew four things: This was the best quiz show I had ever seen. The format would work everywhere. I wanted to get it on ABC and get the rights to it, even though that would be incredibly difficult. And I wanted to quit my job and go produce it."

However, convincing the network brass was quite a different story. But fortunately for Davies, he worked with ABC, struggling at the time in third place, and traditionally lower-ranked networks tend to be the most inventive because they're willing to try anything that might work. Programming head Jamie Tarses and her boss, Stu Bloomberg, agreed to give Davies airtime during August, traditionally the month with the fewest viewers watching, a virtual television programming wasteland.

But never one to be daunted, Philbin saw it as an opportunity to turn a few heads, though he'd admit later he had no idea at the time just how many heads would be turned. Broadcasting a game show in prime time was unusual enough, but ABC went a step further by scheduling all 13 episodes to air over the course of 14 consecutive nights starting August 16, 1999. It would almost be like a *Who Wants to Be a Millionaire?* miniseries. Even though Davies and Philbin were being put out to prime-time pasture, Philbin was up for the challenge. "I think it's exciting TV," Regis said at a press conference, admitting he relished the chance to perform on that part of ABC's schedule that had eluded him for so long: prime time. "It's a challenge of awesome proportions – not even Ted Koppel is on Saturdays and Sundays."

At the July 1999 Television Critics press tour, held in Pasadena, California, Philbin was his usual effacing, upbeat self during the *Who Wants to Be a Millionaire?* presentation. "Hopefully, they won't get sick of me," he joked, referring to being on the air both day and night. He also assured the press that working two shows was not a drain on him physically. "You're talking to an iron man!" Philbin, who turned 66 in 1999, announced. "I'm in the best shape of my life. I've worked with Kathie Lee for 15 years. That builds stamina and endurance. A lesser man would be in his grave by now."

With any game show, probably the hardest part is explaining the concept and trying to make it sound exciting without the benefit of actually playing it. The rules to *Who Wants to Be a Millionaire?* were simple. Through a promotional campaign, ABC would advertise for contestants. Would-be players would call a special toll-free number and answer a series of questions. Their scores would be based on the number of correct answers and on the time it took them to answer. Ultimately, the potential contestants would be flown to New York to attend a taping. Those finalists would then compete against each other to answer one question. The first person to answer the question correctly would then get the opportunity to answer a stack of 15 multiple-choice questions of increasing difficulty on a wide range of topics. The questions would also increase in dollar value, starting at $100 and going to the top prize of $1 million cash. Up to $32,000, a wrong answer would result in the contestant losing all but $1,000.

What adds to the game show's fun and dramatic appeal are the unique safety nets. Contestants get to see each question before deciding whether or not they want to risk their earnings to advance to the next level. Contestants can choose to walk away at any time with what they've won or go for the big money. Then, once a contestant has decided to answer the question, he or she is given three "lifelines" to use in trying to determine the correct answer. The first lifeline is called "50-50" because it eliminates two of the four multiple-choice answers, leaving the contestant with only two choices, one of which is usually obviously correct. The second lifeline is "Ask the Audience." In that case, the player gets to see how the audience members would answer the question. The third lifeline also tends to be the most entertaining. "Phone a Friend" allows the contestant one call, live on television, to either a family member or a friend. Then that person has 30 seconds to listen to the question and tell the player which answer he or she believes to be correct. When asked by a reporter if Kathie Lee would be his Phone a Friend lifeline, Regis laughed. "You must think I just fell off a turnip truck if you think I'm going to answer that."

The description didn't sound like the stuff of programmers' dreams, but Philbin tried to convince the skeptical critics that it was much more intriguing played out than on paper. "Just doubling the money, questions get a little more intense," he told reporters. "But the production values surrounding this is what really is the icing on the cake. The lighting gets a little more intense, the music gets a little stronger, the guy gets up to a quarter-million dollars, suddenly you hear a heartbeat. And then he calls his friend . . . and asks him the question with the four possible answers, and that second hand is ticking, you're down to 16 seconds, the music comes in – I tell you, it's really terrific television."

Producer Davies added, "Monty Hall used to say that every great game show has one moment where the contestant is going to win everything or lose everything. This program takes that moment, heightens it with lighting and music and the intimacy of the set, and plays that moment again and again and again. And it's a very, very simple idea."

The timing of *Who Wants to Be a Millionaire?* couldn't have been more convenient for Regis, who noted that *Live! With Regis & Kathie Lee* would actually be on a hiatus for one of the two weeks the game show would be filming its 13 episodes. When jokingly asked if he'd be giving away his own money, like the Comedy Central game show *Win Ben Stein's Money*, Philbin did a classic double-take and shouted, "I hope not – I hope that's wrong!"

In the other countries where *Who Wants to Be a Millionaire?* had aired, nobody had won the grand prize. "I think the most is 500,000 Australian dollars and Dutch gilders," equivalent to $323,700 and $239,051 U.S. respectively, said Davies. "In Britain, somebody went for 500,000 pounds (sterling), which is more than $800,000 – and got it wrong." As for offering would-be millionaires any advice, Regis said, "I've been poor, and I've been lucky, and frankly, it's better to be lucky."

With the combination of risk, big money, and trivia, the network and the producers were hoping the time was right to revive the popularity of game shows in prime time. "Well, this show I think brings back the excitement and the drama of those quiz shows of the '50s," said producer Vincent Rubino to reporters, "but with the best use of all of the technology in television today." When asked how he'd feel if a lot of the contestants won the $1-million prize, Rubino shrugged. "God bless insurance. That's all I can say."

But even if half the contestants walked away big winners, it would still cost less than what it costs to produce one hour of a dramatic series. In fact, though, only one contestant would get as high as $500,000 over the first 13 episodes, and in total ABC gave away $1.4 million. When you consider it costs FOX about

$3 million to produce an episode of *The X-Files*, programming game shows makes economic sense.

That a show such as *Who Wants to Be a Millionaire?* was a good financial bet was already known. What wasn't expected is that for the two weeks it aired in August it became *the* show everyone was talking about. Not only network executives but also television critics were surprised. "Okay, so *Who Wants to Be a Millionaire?* may not win the prize as best game show ever," wrote *Entertainment Weekly*'s Ken Tucker, who gave the show's first run a B+ rating. "But garishly snazzy *Millionaire* draws you in. You just know that someday, to goose the ratings, Regis is going to strap Kathie Lee down into that chair and ask her to name in descending order the countries with the worst child-labor laws."

Regis counted himself among the pleasantly surprised. "We started out real good, better than expected and then the show just blossomed the longer it was on," Regis says. "We had some really terrific ratings in August. You know, television has given up on the audience in August and the audience has given up on television as well. But here was something new, so frankly, it was easy to get that big rating in August."

But don't let Regis fool you with his downplaying the success of the show. "I remember his face the morning after the first show premiered," says his wife, Joy, "and the ratings were so high. I haven't seen Regis excited like that before."

In the early days, those associated with the show felt compelled to try to explain its appeal. "The calling card is that you can win a million," said cocreator Paul Smith. "But the primary attraction is the drama taking place on a nightly basis. It's seeing people wrestle with some of the most important decisions that they will ever make in their lives. You see them sweating, terrified, biting their nails, their pulse rates high – yet all that's going to happen is they might not go away with as much money as they'd hoped."

As with any new show, *Who Wants to Be a Millionaire?* suffered an embarrassing miscue during its first run. David Honea, a doctoral student in computer engineering from Raleigh, had won $32,000 on ABC's new prime-time show and was going for $64,000 with the question about which of the five Great Lakes is the second largest in area after Lake Superior. Honea said Lake Huron. Regis told him the correct answer was Lake Michigan. Wrong. "A couple of other contestants said, 'You've got to talk to them because you were right,'" he said later at a press interview. After hours of checking and rechecking, Michael Davies told Honea he'd been correct. "He said, 'You don't have to worry. I can tell you right now you've won $64,000 and you are going to get a chance to win from here,'" recalled Honea, who eventually took home winnings of $125,000. "Thank God we pulled it out," Philbin told Claire Bickley of the *Toronto Sun*. "But you know what – we can't do that again. We can't have another screw-up."

The 13-episode run of the show won its time slot, averaging 11.6. During the first week of the run, the show was the second, fifth, sixth, 12th, and 18th most popular show on television. And the ratings for the second week were even higher. The show averaged an 11.6 rating, and by the end of the run 115 million people – nearly half the U.S. population, had seen it. Perhaps best of all, it appealed to young viewers. While game shows rarely appeal to young viewers, *Who Wants to Be a Millionaire?* helped to boost ABC's time-slot performances in the key adults 18-49 demographic by 95% over the previous year – prompting Davies to say to reporters, "The time is right because we have a young audience out there who doesn't remember the 1970s, much less the 1950s."

The response to the show was so unexpected that ABC executives didn't even bother to pretend they knew it would happen all along. "We had confidence in this show," said Stu Bloomberg, cochairman of ABC Television Entertainment

Group. "But I have to admit we were over the moon with its results." Even before the first run had ended, plans were under way to bring the show back for another multinight run for the all-important November sweeps period. "We've captured lightning in a bottle with this show, and we intend to take full advantage of it," Bloomberg said. But then what?

Davies observed to Verne Gay of *Newsday*, "The issue now is, what's best for the show? A lot of people have to worry about what is best for the network, but I think you want *Millionaire* to be something that has potential. There are shows that become franchises and ones that become institutions. My feeling is, I'd like it to be an institution, like *60 Minutes* or *Jeopardy!*" How to achieve that status, he said, is "a high-class problem. You could put it on five nights a week, and it would work, but for how long? Or you could present it as an event, and it could work forever, but maybe not satisfy demand."

Michael Brockman, former chief of daytime and children's schedules for ABC, CBS, and NBC, told Gay that ABC could use *Who Wants to Be a Millionaire?* "once a week, twice or three times a week – it lends itself to that kind of repetition. It's not like you have to mount a situation comedy, so it becomes a very flexible tool for them. But the reason it has worked is because . . . it's very well done. There isn't anything else like it on the air at the moment." But his question, along with that of everyone else, was how the game show would do against *real* competition.

However, before that question could be answered, Davies had to prepare for the next run of shows. And he had to battle controversy that had already reared its snarling head. The first slam against the show was the disproportionate number of male contestants. Of the 130 finalists flown to New York City to appear on the shows, 80% were men. Of the 18 who actually got to play the game, just two were women. Of more concern was that, by Davies's own count, only 3 of the 130 contestants were minorities, and only one made it to the game-playing group.

Then there was the problem with people calling the toll-free number, because in some states would-be contestants had to use a 900 number that cost $1.50 per call. The states requiring use of toll-free numbers for qualifying furnished 82 of the 130 contestants. "It's unfair that there are 900-number states and 800-number states," Davies agreed at a press interview, noting that "house-hopping" was far easier in toll-free locales. "Going into the series, there was no way I could afford to do an 800 number for everybody. But now I hope to find a way."

The issue of gender and race imbalance was more tricky. "If you look at game shows in general, it seems that more men than women apply, especially for the trivia shows. But most of them can take whoever they want to even it out. But our game is a blind selection process. We have no idea whether these people are men or women when they take the phone test. It's something we've got to resolve, but I'm at a little bit of a loss exactly how to do it. On a personal level, I'm someone who believes in affirmative action," he acknowledged. "But on this program, it would be an absolute insult to say the only way we can have minority contestants is to change the selection process so we have a quota. I think that would be horrendous."

His point is that, unlike network casting agents who directly hire the actors, his contestants are picked by a computer based on what they know and how fast they can retrieve it. "We aren't making any intentional effort to choose young, white casts. We are leaving it completely open and democratic. And I don't think we can be faulted on that."

While Davies worked to iron out the kinks of the show, the other networks scrambled to get on the game show money train. "There's no question there's something in the air" making game shows trendy, Leslie Moonves, CEO of CBS Television, told reporters. That "something" meant a sudden interest in all things game showish. "We're sitting on game-show titles that we've had for 10 years and now everybody wants them," said William Morris's Ben Silverman, one of the agents who packaged *Who Wants to Be a Millionaire?* for ABC. CBS Entertainment president Nancy Tellem concurs: "I think *Millionaire* shook up everyone. Now the whole industry is saying 'Wow, we really have to take a closer look,'" she told Jim Jerome of *People*.

Copycats came quickly. First out of the gate was FOX with its obvious rip-off called *Greed*. Soon other shows were in development or production, including updated versions of *What's My Line?*, *Twenty-One*, *The $64,000 Question*, and an adaptation of the popular CD-ROM trivia game, *You Don't Know Jack*, with Paul "Pee-Wee Herman" Reubens as host.

"There certainly is a renewed interest in prime time game shows right now, and I'd be lying if I said it wasn't because of *Who Wants to Be a Millionaire?*," Mike Darnell, head of special programming at FOX, acknowledged to Walt Belcher of the *Tampa Tribune*. "We felt the need to get out there as fast as possible because we think that by the time there's five or six of these on the air, they won't be as special."

But Davies seemed to be unconcerned about those following in his wake. "We were first and I think we've already got people hooked," he told Belcher. "Our big advantage is that unlike other game shows that have an extensive screening process, involving tests and traveling to Los Angeles just to try out, anyone can pick up a telephone and try out." Beyond that, he mentioned to *Dallas Morning News* reporter Ed Bark in September 1999, "There have been so few of these kinds of shows on television lately. And so there are very few people of my generation who know how to produce them. All I've really tried to do is recapture what American television was all about in the first place." Which is obviously a lot more difficult than it sounds.

When it was time to start taping the episodes for the 15-day November run, Philbin was happily cranky about working double duty. "Now we tape *Millionaire* at 7 at night, and guess who's not too happy?" he told reporters. Of course, Regis had never been more happy professionally, though he tried to temper his enthusiasm because, better than anyone involved in *Millionaire*, he knew how television ratings could change overnight. "Maybe *Millionaire* won't be as gigantic a hit in November," he said to *Entertainment Weekly*'s Jess Cagle that month. "August is a pretty easy time. I got lucky with this show. I thought I had climbed my mountain with the morning show. Big hit locally and nationally. And all of a sudden this *Millionaire* show comes along and I'm pushed to another mountain peak. I really don't dare ask anything more. This is it. What else can I want?"

Whatever he might have wished for was probably far exceeded. By the time *Who Wants to Be a Millionaire?* finished its second run, it had averaged 23.8 million viewers a night, easily running away from the competition. It had awarded more than $5 million, including $1 million to one lucky contestant, the largest single game show prize in television history. Not only had it resuscitated the near-death prime-time game show genre, but it had also brought ABC back from the brink of the ratings abyss. "I'm just ready to save the network any time they call," Regis joked with reporters. "I don't know if Regis saved the network," countered Bloomberg, "but he saved my paycheck."

Thinking back on the previous few months, Philbin had the right to gloat a little. "Everybody said, 'Just wait until November when you're up against real competition,'" he recalled. "So November came, there was some real competition – and the ratings were higher! I think it was then we realized, yes indeed, this really is a juggernaut, a phenomenon. That's when it dawned on me we had something really special here." Even so, he admitted, "who knew it was going to be that big? But I'm thrilled that it happened. You wait a lifetime for something like that and sometimes it never happens."

Thinking about his past disappointments and brushes with this kind of celebrity, Philbin told David Bauder of Associated Press, "It's better to be hot. It's fun. I know this business. I was perfectly content with my morning show. People would ask me, 'What's next?' There is nothing next. There are no more mountains for me to climb. Believe me when I tell you, all I wanted when I started this show in 1961 was to be a success nationally." Another time, he mentioned to reporters, "I gotta tell ya, it's a major thrill, after all these years in the trenches, 9 o'clock in the morning with no help, no hype, a phone that doesn't work. It has been a terrific ride. I never had this kind of attention before."

Michael Davies told Lynette Rice of *Entertainment Weekly* that the attention was well deserved. "There's a huge sentiment on staff for Regis," said Davies. "He's been a sidekick and a co-host, but he's never had his own show. There was incredible motivation to make *Millionaire* work, just for him."

Although Philbin also promoted the show as the thing, when pressed by a reporter he suggested his contribution to it. "I bring that element of believability to it, likability. Sometimes big-money shows can be a little bit on the cold side, so I think if you have a host that people like, it helps. This show is serious," he said. "These people are trying to win a lot of money to have it for the first time in their lives. I don't want to intimidate them." But what pleased Regis the most was knowing he was loved by his audience, respected by his peers, and appreciated by his network, to which he remained loyal. "I'm under contract here in the morning, I'm under contract for the night," he said. "I'm taken. My dance card is full."

Of course, not everyone was enthralled with *Who Wants to Be a Millionaire?*, and one of the sharpest criticisms against the show was that the questions were just way too easy, particularly for the lesser amounts of money. Davies thought not. As he mentioned at a press interview, "You know, on most shows, like *Jeopardy*, the greatest lifeline you have is that you don't have to answer the question. On this show, you have to answer every single question. The questions might be easy in their category, but there is such a broad range, it is almost impossible for anybody on a regular basis to be able to go through all the questions in any given stack."

While Regis agreed that "The questions are not impossible," he also thought that "It's the broad range that'll kill you every time." The subject matter of the questions read like a high school curriculum, prompting people to recall state capitals, the world's tallest this or longest that, as well as pop cultural icons. Not nuclear physics or German existential literature but the kind of knowledge of the masses. "I think the success of the show has almost nothing to do with the money whatsoever," Davies suggested. "The million dollars is just a great hook. What works about the show night in and night out is: There are no real people on television apart from this show."

However, winning money is an integral part of the show, and, according to Regis, he gets so nervous it's hard for him to sit there and watch. "It's terribly exciting to be with them as they proceed and progress through the levels. I feel terrible when they lose. For a while, we had a couple of people who just had trouble getting beyond the $1,000 or $2,000 area, and it's a heartbreak, really, literally, for me to have to tell them that yes, indeed, you've lost; you've been reduced down to $1,000. I hate it. I love it when they win and I want more winners and you know, if this thing were so easy, why don't we have more winners? But that's my answer. That's my final answer."

Now, if there is a single indicator of just how deep *Who Wants to Be a Millionaire?* had burrowed into the pop cultural subconsciousness of the viewing public, it was the suddenly ubiquitous catchphrase "Is that your final answer?" In fact, the phrase had been popping up in so many places that the question was posed by a reporter to producer Michael Davies whether he worried that it might become passé. "If you watch the show very closely, we actually edit it [the phrase] out of the first five answers, but not really because I think it's in danger of becoming tired. It's just sort of essential to the format. We don't have a time limit on our show and by not having a time limit, it enables us to have this drama of people changing their minds and sweating and never being quite sure what they're going to do. I simply never want somebody to leave the stage saying, 'Oh, I answered B, but that wasn't my final answer,' so we have to ask, 'Is that your final answer?' I actually think," he added pointedly, "if people would just stop writing about it, I think perhaps it [the question] would sort of go away."

For Regis, the phrase has been both fun and annoying. "It makes people smile to say it. They feel a kinship," he said to Jacques Steinberg. But he revealed that the phrase's beginnings had more to do with legalities than camaraderie – the producers didn't want to be sued by a contestant who claimed that Regis hadn't given him or her a chance to change an answer. But Philbin didn't agree. "I thought we were overdoing it. Still do."

Likewise, competitors thought that ABC was overdoing it by loading the schedule with the show, but ABC refused to apologize. It was trying to figure out the best way to exploit its sizzling hot series. "Every scenario known to man has been thrown out there," said ABC senior vice president Jeff Bader to reporters. "Does it come back as a once-a-week series? Several times a week? An event either in sweeps or once a month? It's just a question of legs. Does the show have legs? And it looks like it does."

And, like Regis, those legs showed no signs of slowing down.

Regis and Joy, 1999

10

Still Around

When *Who Wants to Be a Millionaire?* burned up the ratings in August 1999, it became the talk of Hollywood; when it scorched the competition during the November sweeps, it became a bona fide phenomenon. Suddenly, Regis Philbin was not only the most watched man on television but also the hottest, and everyone wanted a piece of him – or to claim they'd had a piece of him. While he wasn't the same kind of target as Gifford, there were accusations of some skeletons in his closet of a lustier nature.

According to a former stripper named Liz Renay, she and Regis engaged in a one-night stand way back in 1972. Although at 28 years ago this would constitute ancient history for many people, it was still significant because that was just two years after Regis had married Joy. However, at the time, Renay claimed, she had no idea he was married. As she revealed in an exclusive *Globe* interview, she was preparing to write a tell-all book about her top-10 famous lovers and ranked Philbin fourth. "Regis was sweet and cuddly," Liz, then 73, gushed. "I thought if I'd married him and had that kind of sex every night, I'd have been content."

Renay said she met Regis after she was a guest on his show, *Regis Philbin's Saturday Night*, which filmed in St. Louis, to promote her recently published book, *My Face for the World to See*, about her mob ties. Regis apparently asked her if he could come over after the show. They spent a passionate night together, until 4 a.m., when Regis got dressed and left. Needless to say, Philbin's spokesman, Jim Griffin, denied the story.

He also denied another story in which a woman named Marilyn Walsh told reporters Shannon Loughrin and Stephanie Timm of the *Star Magazine* that Regis came on to her during a taping of *Live! With Regis & Kathie Lee*. "Sometimes he'd crouch down next to me, other times he would plop himself in my lap." Walsh said she was waiting to get an autograph after the show and was the last fan there. "All of a sudden, Regis grabbed me and pulled me toward him and tried to kiss me on the mouth." Marilyn said she avoided the kiss and was shocked when Philbin then asked her to meet him in his dressing room in a few minutes. Instead, she left immediately. The *Star* article goes on to quote other women with similar stories.

Ever the realist, Philbin knew this was the price of a certain type of fame. He mentioned at a press interview that "I'm not looking forward to that sort of attention. It's unfortunate, but I guess when you have some kind of success, it automatically turns some people off. Sometimes it develops into a negative situation. It just seems like everyone is waiting to tear you down."

However, unlike the Gifford situation, there were no photos of these alleged incidents. Nor had Regis and Joy ever presented themselves as a golden couple; if anything, despite their good-natured rapport on screen, they managed to convey the difficulties of marriage and the struggle to maintain that rapport. Their revelations about disagreements made them very human. So, even if Regis had a wandering eye, people also believed he really loved Joy and could pass it off as the flirtations of a man of a certain age. After all, it was Regis who had Madonna feel his biceps on *Live! With Regis & Kathie Lee* and asked her, "Tell me the truth – am I an attractive man or not?" (She said yes.) But Joy came across as nobody's fool. If Regis had a fling almost 30 years ago, she would deal with it accordingly, in private. In an irony that would make Kathie Lee cringe, these stories almost seemed to enhance Philbin's mystique. Oh, so he was a dog, but he never pretended to be a saint, and, if he was busted by the tabs, somehow he'd convince everyone it was all a big misunderstanding. Such was the unheralded charm of Regis Philbin.

The success of *Who Wants to Be a Millionaire?* also put a different spin on the perennial question about the future of the Philbin-Gifford duo. Suddenly, instead of focusing on Kathie Lee, the media were now peppering Regis with questions about his future with *Live! With Regis & Kathie Lee* – even though his contract ran through August 2001 and Gifford's was up in July 2000. "Enough with Kathie Lee already!" he said to Lyle V. Harris. "We're going to be on for at least two more years. I consider myself a lucky guy, because no matter what happens with this new show, I'll still be able to go on every morning and talk about whatever I want to for 20 minutes." But Gifford was making her usual comments about how long she'd stay. She was still talking up her proposed sitcom, though she complained to USA *Today*'s Jeannie Williams that it hadn't happened because "everybody wanted to change it," so it was on hold.

But the real question was whether Regis, now the star of a hit prime-time show, would want to leave daytime television behind. When asked by a reporter how it would feel not to go to work with Gifford anymore, Philbin said, "I would miss her terribly. I really would. And I love the freedom of having the first twenty minutes to talk about whatever we want to talk about. There are no writers on that show, as you can tell. So we just are on our own wits out there, and frankly, it's gratifying and satisfying from that point of view. I really haven't made up my mind. I just want to see where this one goes or how many nights they're going to need and then I'll have to weigh what that workload would be against what we're doing in the morning. Kathie Lee isn't worried that I'll be leaving our show. Even if the game show does take off and returns in the fall, I still have a contract that takes me until August 2001, so it's pretty much a ways away."

If Regis did leave the show with Kathie Lee, it wouldn't be because of the physical demands of doing two shows, because the demands weren't all that physical. "On this particular show *(Millionaire)*, really the staff does most of the work. I mean, they fly everybody in; they extract a little biographical information about them, put them on cards. The format, I mean, I know intimately so there's no preparation there. I come here about maybe an hour before show time, change, chat with Michael about what's new and a little bit about the guests that he has briefed earlier in the day, get a kind of fix on them, and then we start the show and it takes on a life of its own. The morning show, I walk over to ABC around 8:20 in the morning, change my clothes. Gelman comes in around 8:45, I talk with him about the guest lineup, check the papers so I know what I did the night before, go down and get made up at ten minutes to 9:00, meet Kathie Lee in the hall at one minute to 9:00, walk down the hallway, walk out as he's introducing us and the show begins."

However, Regis did admit, "I do have a week off and I think, frankly, we could all use it around here. But we have to tape some shows in advance to get that week off. So even though we'll be on three nights a week, I suppose we'll tape five nights a week to make the extra shows so that every now and then there will be a week's off time. And I'll be looking forward to it." As for taking time off *Live! With Regis & Kathie Lee*, though, "I don't know anything about a substitute host – unless you've heard something," he added, laughing.

It seemed as if everything Philbin had ever wanted in his career was finally coming true. Many who knew him at the beginning of his career might have been surprised that he'd come so far as to be honored at the Museum of Television and Radio in late 1999. It was at such moments that Regis gave a rare glimpse into his off-camera side. "I don't like being honored," he admitted humbly at the ceremony. "It makes me uncomfortable."

But not as uncomfortable as *Who Wants to Be a Millionaire?* was making ABC's rivals. Unfortunately, the game show was making some fellow ABC producers feel the heat as well. To make room on the schedule for the multinight run of the game show, ABC juggled its schedule, to the displeasure of other show runners. When the show came back in November, ABC made room on Sunday nights by bumping David E. Kelley's new detective drama *Snoops*, a series that Kelley himself would later cancel. For January 2000, the game show was set to return with an eight-night rollout prior to beginning its new thrice-weekly schedule, airing Tuesdays, Thursdays, and Sundays. But to make room for the show, some other shows had to be moved – or removed. The losers were the series *Oh Grow Up* and *It's Like, You Know. . . .*

Garth Ancier, president of NBC Entertainment, likened ABC's reliance on *Who Wants to Be a Millionaire?* to being addicted to drugs. As he said at a press conference, "It's like crack. Once you're on it, it's wonderful because you get these giant ratings but no one believes it's going to work forever. And the fact is, ABC has taken off a lot of their situation comedies that were in development, a lot of their dramas that were in development to make sure room for these hours and hours of *Millionaire*."

Les Moonves, president and CEO of CBS Television, had his own complaints. "I made a statement a few months ago that every half hour of a game show that's on the air means

100 people in Hollywood are out of work and by that I mean writers, producers, directors. If it (*Millionaire*) expands from three nights to five nights to seven nights, which, judging from these numbers, it very well might, I don't necessarily think that's good for television. I do hope the genre slows down. I don't think it's necessarily good to have a proliferation of it. Is it like a drug? Well, it's not quite as damaging, but almost."

ABC's Stu Bloomberg noted, "I think it's an unfortunate analogy that he (Ancier) chose. I don't believe we are mortgaging our future at all. We are eternally grateful to have this wonderful show." When asked if the show would move to seven nights a week, as Moonves suggested, Bloomberg shook his head. "No. We really like the three-night schedule. We did extensive research before making this decision and people really wanted to see it more than one night a week."

For the most part, Philbin just sat back at a safe distance and let the network executives go at each other. However, he did express remorse over one thing Moonves said. "I never expected – I don't think any of us did – that we would be putting some shows out of commission because they wanted more than once a week. I know what it is like to be out of work and I feel for those people. But what are we going to do? The network is saying more, more, more and we are trying to give it to them."

Not surprisingly, some media and academic pundits pointed to the proliferation of game shows as yet another example of the decline of Western civilization. Davies was obviously weary of the rap. "The idea that television is being junked up is ridiculous," he said to reporters. "Compare this to all the crap sitcoms that have come on for the past 10 years." As far as Davies is concerned, *Who Wants to Be a Millionaire?* is more educational, dramatic, and positive than the vast majority of programming. "I find it appalling every time a professor of television at Syracuse University says this is a sign of the dumbing down of America. I think it's a sign of the dumbing down of

America that there are professors of television at major universities."

Davies found a soulmate in former political consultant and current game show host Ben Stein. "The drama on television at this point is so pitifully synthetic that the only real drama is on the quiz show," said Stein, host of *Win Ben Stein's Money*, Comedy Central's second-highest-rated program. "People are terribly keyed up. The people I shake hands with after each round, their hands are soaking wet. I've seen grown men, repeatedly, cry after shows. And that's only for 5,000 bucks."

Although many in Hollywood expressed their hopes that game shows are a passing fancy, Davies thinks they might be around for a while, especially in light of the advances being made in interactive television. As he noted at a press interview, "Perhaps it doesn't last on television forever, but you know what? It really could be the first program in the whole new programming platform. I love Virtual Regis. I think that's a great idea. We're working very hard on developing the interactive and Internet side of this thing. I think that in television, it's tough to find examples of really well-thought-out, well-produced television programs that just disappear immediately. I know there has been much said about this being crack cocaine or about this being addictive, but I guess I don't see it in such terms. I just see it as being a really solid idea for a television program that a lot of people who watch it can relate to. It's worked everywhere around the world where it's been on and I think it could definitely have some legs."

Even NBC's Ancier had to acknowledge, "*Jeopardy!* and *Wheel of Fortune* have been dominant shows in syndication for ten years and they've sustained themselves. Most people say they watch them because they think they're learning new things; they think they're getting smarter. . . . So you can find that there's a certain balance of game shows and audience for them that's going to continue to work."

In other words, it was conceivable that *Who Wants to Be a Millionaire?* could have as long a run as, say, *Sixty Minutes* or *Gunsmoke.* It's therefore a good thing Regis likes game shows. "I saw them all," he said, smiling. "Years ago I enjoyed *What's My Line?* and *To Tell the Truth.* I loved them for their simplicity and the fun they produced. I guess I was a fan then. Of course, they went out of favor and I kind of lost track of them. But it wasn't until I saw *Who Wants to Be a Millionaire?* that I got excited about game shows again."

Even though the show's millionaires have been few and far between, the London-based underwriting firm Goshawk Syndicate decided to sue Buena Vista Entertainment, which produces the game show, demanding the show ask harder questions and select dumber contestants – but ABC responded by saying it wasn't about to change a winning formula. Under its contract, Goshawk is required to pay out prize money to contestants who win $500,000 or more after a deductible of $1.5 million is met. The contract contains a $5-million ceiling, meaning the insurance company would have to shell out to a maximum of five $1-million winners. Of the 51 shows so far, only an Internal Revenue Service agent and a Miami attorney have won the top prize by answering 15 questions correctly. Three other contestants have won $500,000 each. But the insurance company is worried the American numbers could mount, predicting "substantial losses" in the lawsuit filed in Britain's High Court. The suit demanded that the producers make "significant changes" in the difficulty of the questions and in how they select contestants.

"Unquestionably, the integrity of the show is above reproach and nobody is claiming otherwise," ABC spokeswoman Julie Hoover said in a press release. "This is simply a dispute in which the company providing insurance is trying to get out of coverage on the basis of a conversation it had with a broker."

While Goshawk was shelling out money to winning contestants, Regis was raking it in. At the January 2000 Television

Critics Press Tour, Regis was asked if he'd received any token of appreciation from ABC, such as the Porsches that NBC had given the previous year to the *Will and Grace* cast. Philbin assumed his put-upon-guy voice and said dryly, "Regis is lucky he got a tie!" Well, in February 2000, ABC's parent company, Disney, made sure he could buy a boatload of ties when it renegotiated his contract to give him an annual salary of $20 million, unprecedented for a game show host. The deal would also extend his run as the cohost of *Live! With Regis & Kathie Lee.* "They're working on finishing up the details of a new contract," Philbin told the *New York Post* on February 28, 2000. "Because I only have a year and a half left on the old contract, I think it might be like a joint situation – where I have to extend the morning show to satisfy the commitment I've made for *Millionaire*." What most viewers and people within the television industry knew was that Philbin had been working under a temporary agreement signed the previous summer that paid him a reported $100,000 a show. "This is something new for me," he said at a press conference of the accolades and money being thrown at him. "I did Atlantic City recently, at the Resorts Hotel, and, gosh, the shows were totally sold out, with 300 people turned away at the door. And that's a big house, with 1,500 seats." Then he added, "My free time is not what it used to be."

After all those years wondering where the next job was coming from to pay the mortgage and buy the food, Regis was truly getting paid like a king. And, expectedly, it made him more humble than ever. "I guess I've been around too long, and especially with these same people, that they treat me the same way and I don't have any complaints about that," he said when asked if people were acting differently toward him. "You know, the real star of this show, frankly, is the show and what they do with the lights and music and the production and the million dollars, as I said before. The million dollars is the lynchpin of this show. For years being a millionaire in this country was what everybody wanted to become and here's the chance to do it on television in one night. And it's very exciting, so basically that is the star and the thrust of the show."

If that was true, then Regis was positively basking in the glow. In a knee-deep irony, he'd become television's latest fashion statement, with his signature monochromatic shirt and tie that retail stores realized were suddenly the rage. (Or, we could say, the *Reege.*) "They're jumping on it," Tim Leamy, co-owner of Sebastian's Closet, a source of sophisticated men's style in Dallas, told Rob Brinkley of the *Dallas Morning News.* "Retailers are going so far as to call their newest dark ties 'the Regis tie,' or a line of clothes 'the Regis line.' It's definitely out there. The look worn by Regis the night before is the first thing to sell out the next morning."

Lou Melazzo, general manager of Beau Brummel, the New York retailer that provides Philbin's on-air wardrobe, told Holly Hanson of Knight Ridder Newspapers, "We get e-mail every day from people who want those shirts and ties," he said. "He's really put men's wear on the map again, and it's nice. It's refreshing to have people go back to some elegance again."

That sentiment was dittoed by Gregg Andrews, fashion director for Nordstrom's Central States region. "We find that we are getting requests for that look at least once a day, with direct reference to Regis Philbin. We're getting the requests from guys in their late 20s on up. I can see him being a fashion icon for people in his age range, but he is that for younger people as well." The shirt-and-tie combos in gray or blue were the most in demand, though one of Philbin's earliest statements – black suit, black shirt, and shiny black tie – was also popular. Ironically, Philbin initially balked at the black-on-black-on-black look. "This isn't *The Sopranos*," he said before giving in.

With all the hoopla over the "Regis look," a clothing line was inevitable. At a press conference held in New York, it was announced that Van Heusen would make matching shirts and ties under the Regis name in "a multimillion, multiple-year deal." The line would roll out by Labor Day, with the shirt sets selling for about $40. Intent on not following in Kathie Lee's sweatshop footsteps, Philbin made it clear that he'd looked into working conditions for the makers of his line. "That's the *first* thing I did! That ain't going to happen to me!"

However, Regis found himself in the middle of a less issue-related controversy with a rival game show host, *Jeopardy!*'s Alex Trebek, after Trebek dissed *Who Wants to Be a Millionaire?* for asking questions such as "What's the usual color of Post-its?" Philbin retorted to the press, "Once and for all, I think it is time to show America how much you know. We'll take you out to dinner. We'll have some laughs. And then we'll put you in the hot seat, and we'll see if you know the color of Post-its."

Perhaps Trebek was just miffed at a previous outburst from Regis, who told Verne Gay of *Newsday* that his game show was "bigger than *Wheel*! Bigger than *Jeopardy!* I think it can give *Jeopardy!* a good run for its money. What does Alex Trebek do? Give out a couple dollars. I don't want to be Alex Trebek. He can hardly get through the questions," Philbin said, before adding, "I'm kidding. I can see what's happening here: You're going to write 'Regis Hates Trebek. . . .'"

Regis may have been kidding, but Trebek seemed to be serious when he told Alan James Frutkin of the *Washington Post* that some *Jeopardy!* fans complained that the networks' huge payoffs in fact cheapen knowledge. "If somebody can win that much money for what the viewer considers to be a real easy response, then there's something not quite right," Trebek said, adding, "Our contestants make money the old-fashioned way – they earn it."

Perhaps all the excitement of hosting two shows and bickering with Trebek was too much for Regis, because in late April he was back in the hospital. After returning from a vacation at Donald Trump's Florida estate, he felt familiar chest pains and immediately checked himself into a hospital. "I had a choice of treatment by medication for several months – or an atherectomy, which took only a half-hour. I decided on the latter procedure," which Regis reported in a press release was basically a cleaning out of the inside of an artery that supplies blood to the heart. In other words, it was a mild version of the angioplasty he'd had years earlier.

While Regis's heart may have been intact, the hearts of millions of *Live! With Regis & Kathie Lee* fans were broken when Kathie Lee surprised viewers by announcing on February 29, 2000, that she'd leave the show when her contract expired at the end of July. The timing was interesting considering that Regis had just been made ABC's $20-million man. Gifford said that a decade and a half of hosting duties was more than enough and that her reason for not renewing her contract was to spend more time with her family. "It's the day you have been praying for for 15 years," Gifford joked with Philbin.

As expected, many in the media suggested that she was quitting more out of a snit over Regis's tremendous success with the game show. Others wondered if she was jealous or wanted out so she could prove to everyone she could be equally successful on her own in her long-talked-about sitcom. Whatever her motives, this time she was serious. But what was once thought of as a possible death knell for the talk show suddenly turned into an opportunity. Like the majority of talk shows, *Live! With Regis & Kathie Lee* had suffered a ratings decline and was down 10% from 1999. With Regis on top of the television world, perhaps new blood could rejuvenate the show. Instead of reacting to Gifford's announcement with trepidation, many at the talk show felt invigorated.

"Obviously, she's not irreplaceable," Art Moore, the executive in charge of the show's production, was quoted as saying in the *St. Louis Post-Dispatch* by Gail Pennington. "We'll just go in another direction. We'll find someone Regis clicks with." In short, they'd look "for a new co-host who will preserve the show's chemistry."

But while everyone seemed to be looking ahead, Pennington asked viewers, and the industry, to take a look back. "Picture Regis, if he'd never met Kathie Lee, as a third-tier performer in Las Vegas, opening for magicians and animal acts. At Oscar time, he'd be on the sidewalk with a microphone, interviewing arrivals for an obscure basic cable channel. Picture Kathie Lee, if Regis had never entered her life, hawking albums on late-night TV and doing dinner theater in Secaucus, N.J. Instead of filling in for Letterman, she'd be filling in for Andy Williams in Branson. Without each other, however, it's highly doubtful that either would have reached this point. Despite the spin they're putting on it now, Regis will miss Kathie Lee. Kathie Lee will miss Regis. And morning TV will miss that something they had together."

Of course, news of Kathie Lee's departure was almost immediately overshadowed by the question of who would replace her. There was no shortage of volunteers boldly announcing they'd like to be in the running. According to an AP wire story, CNBC financial reporter Maria Bartirimo told *People* she'd consider giving up Wall Street if presented with the chance to work alongside Philbin on the morning show. "It would take a phenomenal position for me to consider leaving, and that's how I feel about the Kathie Lee spot."

Cybill Shepherd told practically anyone who'd listen that she'd "consider it a great privilege" to replace Kathie Lee. Cybill was quoted in the *New York Post* as saying, "I adore Regis. He's one of the funniest, warmest and best people who have ever been on television."

After Lisa Ling of *The View* announced that she, too, would like to replace Gifford, Florence Henderson countered in a press interview with the comment, "I'd be better than Lisa Ling," adding playfully, "I don't think they should bring in someone too young, because it makes Regis look really old. Regis is a tough curmudgeon. I'm just the opposite, and I'm funny."

Almost everyday another name was mentioned, and a report claimed Regis had asked his original cohost, Cyndy Garvey, to try out for the job. Among others mentioned were Linda Dano, Joan Lunden, Leeza Gibbons, Cindy Crawford, and even Susan Lucci. But in a number of polls taken, the person the audience wanted to see was none other than Joy Philbin. However, on July 5, 2000, Joy put the idea to pasture. Filling in for Gifford, she told the audience that, despite being very flattered by the interest in her, she thought it best for her marriage that she remain the occasional fill-in host and not be a permanent fixture. Regis looked on with interest, having previously said he truly didn't know whether Joy wanted to be seriously considered for the job or not.

With Joy out of the running, the decision really comes down to Regis. "Regis will have a major voice in the decision," agent Ed Hookstratten was quoted in *Variety* as saying, as reported by *People Daily Online*. "He's at the top of the heap with his career . . . and he'll have a major role [in the decision]. I think he's earned that voice." Another source was quoted by *People Daily Online* as saying, "This is an important franchise to the company, and all the ABC-owned stations air it. It's all going to come down to who has that little spark of magic that works with Regis."

But who can keep up with the man who's at the top of his professional and personal life just a few years shy of 70? In many ways, Regis is timeless, a product of almost every generation he has entertained. His durability is unquestioned. "Regis has that very rare ability to be himself on camera," says his producer and protégé Michael Gelman. "He can look through the camera and connect with the viewer at home."

And that's no small thing, though to Regis Philbin small is the key. As he said in a press interview, "I started small and learned to keep it small. Small is friendlier and more real. Small lasts longer. It wears well. I guess that's why I'm still around."

Works Cited

(*Note:* In addition to the sources listed below, wire service items, press interviews, and press releases have been used extensively, especially in chapters 9 and 10.)

Bark, Ed. "Behind the Screens: A Talk-Show Tour of the Big Apple." *Dallas Morning News* 9 Nov. 1997: 1C.

——. "*Millionaire* Not on Easy Street Yet." *Dallas Morning News* 5 Sept. 1999: 1C.

——. "Pal Joey: The Rat Pack's Sole Survivor Revels in Memories, Recounts His Role as the Glue that Kept the Swingers Tight." *Dallas Morning News* 16 Aug. 1998: 1C.

"Bartirimo Seeks Kathie Lee's Spot." *AP Online* 30 Mar. 2000. <www.ap.org/index.html>.

Bauder, David. "Late-Career Success Delights *Millionaire* Host Regis Philbin." *Dallas Morning News* 7 Nov. 1999: 5C.

Belcher, Walt. "TV Greed: Viewers and Networks Alike Lick Their Lips over the Huge Profits of *Who Wants to Be a Millionaire?* and Its Game Show Successors." *Tampa Tribune* 2 Nov. 1999: 1.

Bickley, Claire. "You're Playing Regis' Game." *Toronto Sun* 31 Oct. 1999: TV3.

Bonheim, Susan. Letter. *People* 25 Aug. 1986: 4.

Brinkley, Rob. "The Rich Look of Regis: Men Emulate the Game-Show Host's Winning Wardrobe." *Dallas Morning News* 12 Apr. 2000: 6E.

Broeske, Pat H., et al. "News and Notes: Flashes." *Entertainment Weekly* 22 Apr. 1994: 12.

Cagle, Jess. "In Regis We Trust." *Entertainment Weekly* 5 Nov. 1999: 25.

——. "Kathie Lee's Hair Trigger: Why Has Gifford Turned Snippy on Live with Regis and Kathie Lee?" *Entertainment Weekly* 24 June 1994: 20.

——. "'Live' Wire after 30 Years in the Biz, Regis Philbin Is Happy and Hyper in the Big Time." *Entertainment Weekly* 24 July 1992: 28.

——. "Real Live." *Entertainment Weekly* 5 Apr. 1991: 8.

——. "Regis and Kathie Lee and Michael." *Entertainment Weekly* 19 July 1991: 44.

——. "Regis Philbin's Other Better Half Comfort and Joy." *Entertainment Weekly* 15 Apr. 1994: 48.

Cannon, Bob. "Music Features: The Lost Philbin Tapes Out of His Rege." *Entertainment Weekly* 20 May 1994: 62.

Cannon, Damian. "Movie Reviews." U.K. 1997. <www.imdb.com>.

Carswell, Sue. "At Ease: On the Sidelines with . . . Regis Philbin. At His Beloved Notre Dame, the TV Host Gets His Irish Up for a Big Game." *People* 6 Dec. 1993: 154.

Castro, Peter. "Chatter: Baby Talk." *People* 29 Jan. 1990: 94.

Chadakoff, Rochelle. "With the New Kathie Lee Gifford Label, Wal-Mart Works on Its Fashion Image." *Newsday* 2 Mar. 1995: B17.

Clarke, Norm. "Talk of the Town." *Denver Rocky Mountain News* 15 Dec. 1997: 6A.

Coutros, Evonne E. "Regis Is on the Loose." *Record* [Bergen County, NJ] 5 Nov. 1993: 019.

"Cybill Steps Up." *New York Post* 20 Apr. 2000. <www.nypost.com>.

"Daddy Dearest: Regis Philbin Treated Son like a Leper, Ex-Teacher Charges." *Globe* 26 Mar. 1996.

Derdarin, Christine. "Mail: Regis and Kathie Lee." Letter. *People* 21 Oct. 1991: 6.

Deutsch, Peggy. Letter. *People* 23 June 1997: 4.

Dumas, Andrea H. Letter. *People* 23 June 1997: 4.

Eftimiades, Maria. "Soap Star Andrea Evans Quit Her Job and Left New York to Escape a Madman." *People* 17 May 1993: 66.

Eisenberg, Lawrence. "Kathie Lee Gifford: 'I Have to Keep Growing.'" *Good Housekeeping* 1 May 1994: 161+.

Epstein, Kathie. *The Quiet Riot.* Old Tappan, NJ: Revell, 1971.

Ethnic NewsWatch © SoftLine Information, Inc., Stamford, CT.

"EW Poll: Crazy for Kathie Lee." *Entertainment Weekly* 26 Jan. 1996: 14.

Fairley, Juliette. "Things Have Changed at Cardinal Hayes: But Support for the Small." *Black Enterprise* 30 Sept. 1995.

Frutkin, Alan James. "Answer: It All Depends; Question: Will the *Millionaire* Craze Spoil *Jeopardy!*?" *Washington Post* 2 Apr. 2000: Y07.

Gatti, Alice. "Mail: Picks and Pans." Letter. *People* 26 Sept. 1988: 8.

Gay, Verne. "Regis Gets Quizzical: Just Don't Call His New Gig a Game Show if You Want the Cash." *Newsday* 12 Aug. 1999: B35.

——. "$*M*A*$*H: There's Still Cash in *Millionaire*, but Where?" *Newsday* 30 Aug. 1999: B03.

Gifford, Kathie Lee, with Jim Jerome. *I Can't Believe I Said That! An Autobiography.* Rev. ed. New York: Pocket, 1993.

Gleick, Elizabeth, and Sue Carswell. "Regis's Sidekick Says Her Life Hasn't Been All Party, No Pain." *People* 2 Nov. 1992: 122.

Goodman, Mark, and Lyndon Stambler. "Strictly Maternal: Porn King Larry Flynt Is Hustling a Wholesome New Magazine – for Mothers-to-Be." *People* 2 Aug. 1993: 91.

Good Morning America. 3 Feb. 1993.

Greenblatt, Stuart. "Mail: Picks and Pans." *People* 26 Sept. 1988: 8.

Green, Mary, and Terry Kelleher. "*Picks and Pans: Tube.*" *People* 8 Sept. 1997: 15.

Handy, Bruce. "And Then There Was One." 6 July 1998. <www.timo.com>.

Hanson, Holly. *Knight Ridder Newspapers* 9 Apr. 2000.

Hard Copy. 9 Feb. 1995.

Harris, Lyle V. "Enough about Kathie Lee . . . Regis Looks like a Million Bucks." *Atlanta Constitution* 16 Aug. 1999: C1.

Hellmich, Nanci. "Radu Sees Exercise as Life Enhancement." *usa Today* 19 July 1996: 04D.

"How He Mended Fences with Son and Daughter." *Globe Magazine* 18 Jan. 2000: 37.

"It's Nice to Be Vindicated." *People* 7 Mar. 1994: 270.

Jarvis, Jeff. "Picks and Pans: Tube." *People* 5 Sept. 1988: 15.

Jerome, Jim. "The Many Faces of Kathy Lee." *Ladies Home Journal* 1 Sept. 1994: 164+.

Jerome, Jim, with Glenn Garelik. "Love that Tender! What's the Final Answer Backstage at *Who Wants to Be a Millionaire*? White Knuckles, Wild Guesses, Technical Glitches – and One Happy Host Named Regis." *People* 22 Nov. 1999: 72+.

The Joey Bishop Show. 26 Dec. 1969. abc.

Kitman, Marvin. "Kathie Lee Shipping Out?" *Newsday* 3 Dec. 1995: 21.

Kubasik, Ben. "Regis Philbin Is Hospitalized." *Newsday* 14 May 1993: 116.

Kuklenski, Valerie. "Kathie Lee Backlash." United Press International. 23 Nov. 1995. pr Newswire.

Leonard Maltin's Movie and Video Guide. <www.imdb.com>.

"Letters: Host with the Most." *Time* 22 Nov. 1993: 6.

Letter to the editor. *Los Angeles Times* 22 Nov. 1993.

Lipton, Michael A., and Nancy Matsumoto. "Reege's Man of the Hour for Comic Relief: Regis and Kathie Lee Find a Foil in Producer Michael Gelman." *People* 22 May 1995: 53+.

Live! With Regis & Kathie Lee. 8 May 1991.

——. 31 Aug. 1992.

——. 13 May 1993.

——. 23 May 1994.

——. 25 May 1994.

——. 5 July 2000.

"Live! With Regis & Kathie Lee." <www.wchs.com>. [WCHS-TV8 Web site].

Long, Tom. "Egregious and Kathie Lee." *Gannett News Service* 21 May 1997.

Loughrin, Shannon, and Stephanie Timm. "Regis Won't Take No for His Final Answer." *Star Magazine* n.d.

"Mail: Kathie Lee Gifford." *People* 23 Nov. 1992: 4.

Martone, Diana. "Mail: Chatter." Letter. *People* 19 Feb. 1990: 4.

McDougal, Dennis. "R.I.P. for *A.M.L.A.*" *Los Angeles Times* 24 Sept. 1991: F1, 12.

Novak, Ralph, Ken Gross, and Joanne Kaufman. "Picks and Pans: Pages." *People* 7 Aug. 1989: 25.

"Oh, Reege, What a Lover!" *Globe* 17 Aug. 1999.

Oldenburg, Ann. "Regis' Personal Link to Rehabilitation Cause." *USA Today* 22 Sept. 1997: 02D.

Park, Jeannie, and Maria Eftimiades. "Happy: Kathie Lee and Frank Gifford Finally Make It a Threesome." *People* 21 May 1990: 162.

Pennington, Gail. "With Regis and Kathie Lee, It's Textbook TV Chemistry: Separately, They're Ordinary. Together, They're Winners. And Their Tale Shows How Good Pairing Can Equal Success on the Tube and in Real Life." *St. Louis Post-Dispatch* 5 Mar. 2000: F3.

——. "Yakety-Yak Talk Show Overload Leaves a Couch Potato's Eyes Glazed Over." *St. Louis Post-Dispatch* 12 Nov. 1993: 01G.

People Daily Online 12 Apr. 2000. <www.people.com/daily>.

"The Permanent Second Fiddles." *Newsweek* 1 Sept. 1969: 45.

Philbin, Regis. Interview with Marion Long. <www.homearts.com>.

——. Interview with Paul Harris. *Harris Online Interviews* 22 July 1997. <www.harrisonline.com>.

——. *Harris Online Interviews* 4 Dec. 1997. <www.harrisonline.com>.

——. "A Private Talk with Regis." With Larry Eisenberg. *Good Housekeeping* May 1992: 179.

Philbin, Regis, with Bill Zehme. *I'm Only One Man.* New York: Hyperion, 1995.

Potok, Mark. "Insulted Elmo Cancels Regis' Appearance." usa *Today* 20 Dec. 1996: 03D.

Powell, Joanna. "Up with Kathie Lee." *Redbook* July 1992: 80.

Powers, William. "Media Rex." *New Republic* 9 June 1997.

Press, Eyal. "No Sweat: The Fashion Industry Patches Its Image." *Progressive* 1 Sept. 1996: 30+.

"Regis' Lonely Ex Lives in Poverty." *Globe* 27 Feb. 1996: 20.

Regis Uncensored: His Amazing Life from Rags to Millions. American Media Specials magazine 28 Mar. 2000.

Rice, Lynette, with Dan Snierson. "The Latest News from the tv Beat." *Entertainment Weekly* 3 Dec. 1999: 82.

Richman, Alan. "Host: Chow, Darling, and Cue the Carrots! A Critic Turns the Tables on Celeb Restaurateurs from Sonny to Charo." *People* 19 Dec. 1988: 154.

Rist, Curtis. "Trouble: Out of Control, Angry, and Troubled, Cyndy Garvey Is Accused of Harassment." *People* 18 Mar. 1996: 69+.

Rosenthal, Phil. "Talking Tough." *Daily News* [Los Angeles], Life Section, 17 May 1994: 1+.

Rudolph, Ileane. "tv's Funniest Squabbling Couple Get Revved Up for Their Big Night Out." *tv Guide* 7 – 13 Sept. 1991: 16–17.

Ryan, Joan. "Why Sports Heroes Abuse Their Wives." *Redbook* 1 Sept. 1995: 83+.

"Sad, Lonely Life of Ex-Wife." *Globe Magazine* 18 Jan. 2000: 36.

Scaduto, Anthony, et al. "Inside New York." *Newsday* 14 Sept. 1992: 13.

——. "Inside New York." *Newsday* 18 Nov. 1992: 13.

Schleier, Curt. "While It's Difficult to Say Exactly What It Is that Philbin Does, Viewers Love It – and Him." *Minneapolis Star Tribune* 10 June 1996: 08E.

Schwarzbaum, Lisa. "Entertainment Tonight Ten from the Hart." *Entertainment Weekly* 19 June 1992: 58.

Shain, Michael, and Pat Wechsler. "Inside New York." *Newsday* 10 Nov. 1993: 13.

Smith, Alan. "Kathie Lee and the Abortion Bomber." *National Enquirer* 8 June 1999. <www.nationalenquirer.com>.

Smith, Connie. "Mail: Regis and Kathie Lee." Letter. *People* 21 Oct. 1991: 6.

Smith, Liz. "Goodbye, Kathie Lee?" *Newsday* 27 Oct. 1995: A13.

Sporkin, Elizabeth, and Sue Carswell. "Can They Talk! When Regis Philbin and Kathie Lee Gifford Start, There's No Telling Where They Will Stop." *People* 30 Sept. 1991: 34.

"Spotlite." *Denver Rocky Mountain News* 18 Mar. 1998: 2D.

Stanton, J. Letter. *People* 23 June 1997: 4.

Starr, Michael. "Final Answer? Could Be $20M for Regis." *New York Post* 28 Feb. 2000. <www.nypost.com>.

Steinberg, Jacques. "We Haven't Heard the Last of 'Final Answer?'" *Dallas Morning News* 9 Dec. 1999: 7C.

Taaffe, William. "Television: 'Tis the Season for Heidi to Spread Her Cheers and Jeers." *Sports Illustrated* 26 Dec. 1988: 10.

Thomas, Karen. "Gelman, a Go-to Kind of Guy: Getting Grief Brings Life to Live." *USA Today* 25 May 1994: 1.

Tracy, Kathleen. "Regis' Daughter Trapped in Booze and Drug Hell." *Globe* 7 Sept. 1993.

Tucker, Ken. "On the Money: *Who Wants to Be a Millionaire?* Everyone, It Seems, from the Response to This U.K. Game-Show Import." *Entertainment Weekly* 3 Sept. 1999: 49.

——. "Television Live with Regis and Kathie Lee Syndicated Daily." *Entertainment Weekly* 14 Sept. 1990: 7.

Wasserman, Elizabeth. "The Contenders: Even 9-Year-Olds Flock to Atlantic City, Hoping Someday They'll Walk on Air, Too." *Newsday* 22 Sept. 1992: 42.

Williams, Jeannie. "Costner Stands Up for Kathie Lee." *USA Today* 2 Mar. 1999: 02D.

Witchel, Alex. "Regis Philbin: On Top of the World, and Loving/Hating It." *Minneapolis Star Tribune* 6 Nov. 1999: 06E.

Wright, Ricky. Rev. of *It's Time for Regis*, by Regis Philbin. <www.amazon.com>.

Wulf, Steve, ed. "Scorecard: Couldn't Put It Down." *Sports Illustrated* 29 Feb. 1988: 15.

Zehme, Bill. "It's Reege's World: We Just Live in It." *Esquire* 1 June 1994: 80+.

——. "The Sidekick Inside Me: A Journalist's Attempt to Become a Talk Show Host Sidekick." *Esquire* 1 June 1997: 60+.